The Furthest Shore

To Dominique, Yvan and Leonel

The
Furthest
Shore

Images of Terra Australis from

the Middle Ages to Captain Cook

William Eisler

CAMBRIDGE
UNIVERSITY PRESS

Published by the Press Syndicate of the University of Cambridge
The Pitt Building, Trumpington Street, Cambridge CB2 1RP, UK
40 West 20th Street, New York, NY 10011–4211, USA
10 Stamford Road, Oakleigh, Melbourne 3166, Australia

994. 01 E15

Printed in Hong Kong by Colorcraft

National Library of Australia cataloguing-in-publication data

Eisler, William Lawrence, 1948– .
The furthest shore.
Includes index.
1. Voyages and travels in art. 2. Australia in art. 3. Pacific
Area in art. 4. Graphic arts – Europe – History – 16th century.
5. Graphic arts – Europe – History – 17th century. 6. Graphic
arts – Europe – History – 18th century. 6. Art – Psychology. I.
Title.
760.044999

Library of Congress cataloguing-in-publication data

Eisler, William Lawrence, 1948– .
The furthest shore: images of Terra Australis from the Middle
Ages to Captain Cook / William Eisler.
Includes bibliographical references and index.
1. Australia – Discovery and exploration – Pictorial works –
Exhibitions. 2. Australia – Pictorial works – Exhibitions.
I. Title.
DU93.E365 1995   94–4178
994.01–dc20   CIP

A catalogue record of this book is available from the British Library.

ISBN 0 521 39268 3 Hardback

Contents

I The Invention of a Southern Continent

II The Southern World in the Age of Dutch Expansion: 1606–1756

Figures

Plates

A Chronology

of the Southland

5th century BC	Pythagoras devises his concept of southern landmasses, counterbalancing those of the northern parts of the world.
2nd century BC–1st century AD	Further references to a southern world in the writings of Crates of Mallos, Pomponius Mela and Ptolemey.
5th century AD	Macrobius in his *Dream of Scipio* evokes the image of an uninhabited southern world.
8th century AD	Commentary to the Apocalypse of St John by Beatus of Liébana inspires maps which depict an austral region.
Early 14th century	Earliest known manuscripts of Marco Polo's travel account, describing the legendary southern realms of Beach, Lucach and Maletur, which would be incorporated into an imaginary Terra Australis on maps of the Renaissance.
1488	Portuguese reach the Cape of Good Hope.
1498	Portuguese reach India.
1501–1502	Amerigo Vespucci, in his third voyage to South America, arrives in what he describes as the 'antipodes'.
1512	Voyage of Portuguese explorer Francisco Rodrigues, who arrives in Banda, East Indies.
1519–1522	Magellan's global voyage. Tierra del Fuego now forms the northern boundary of the imaginary Terra Australis.
1526	Discovery of New Guinea by Jorge de Ménesès.
1529–1530	Voyage of Jean Parmentier to Sumatra inspires the legend of southern continent, Java la Grande, depicted on French maps until 1566.
1541	World map of Gerard Mercator establishes parameters of a massive Terra Australis, covering the southern portion of the globe and incorporating the lands mentioned by Marco Polo. This image would remain largely unaltered throughout the sixteenth century, although contradicted by later discoveries, notably those of Drake.
1567–1569	First expedition of Alvaro de Mendaña y Neyra, in search of legendary islands west of South America; discovery of Solomon Islands in Melanesia.

1577–1580	Sir Francis Drake's circumnavigation indicates no austral region lying below South America.
1595–1597	Second Mendaña expedition, in search of Terra Australis; discovery of the Marquesas (Polynesia).
1605–1606	Voyage of Willem Jansz to New Guinea and Cape York on behalf of the Dutch East India Company; first European landing on Australian continent.
1605–1607	Voyage of Pedro Fernández de Quirós and Luis Váez de Torres discovers La Austrialia del Espíritu Santo (Vanuatu), thought to be part of Terra Australis. In 1606 Torres becomes the first European to sail through the strait which would later bear his name, and most probably comes within sight of Cape York.
1615–1617	Voyage of Jacob le Maire and Willem Schouten in search of Terra Australis; discovery of Futuna and Tonga.
1623	Voyage of the *Pera* and *Arnhem* under Jan Carstensz to Cape York and the Gulf of Carpentaria: first expedition to explore the Australian interior.
1618–1628	Dutch discoveries in the western half of Australia, recorded systematically on the map by Hessel Gerritsz.
1642–1643	First voyage of Abel Tasman to the Southland; reaches Tasmania, New Zealand, Fiji, Tonga, New Ireland, northern New Guinea.
1642–1643	Voyage of Hendrik Brouwer on behalf of the Dutch West India Company marks the final attempt to locate Terra Australis south of the Americas.
1644	Tasman explores the northern coast of Australia, and the Gulf of Carpentaria.
1645–1646	World map of Joan Blaeu records Tasman's discoveries in Australia ('New Holland'). In spite of Torres's discoveries, Australia and New Guinea remained linked together on Dutch maps.
1688	William Dampier arrives on the northwest shores of Australia.
1696–1697	Expedition of Willem de Vlamingh to the west coast of Australia.
1699–1700	Second voyage of Dampier, to Australia and New Britain.
1705	Voyage of Maarten van Delft to northeastern Arnhem Land.
1705	Voyage of Jacob Weyland to New Guinea (Geelvinck Bay); captive Papuans sent to Java and Amsterdam. First images of wallabies drawn, by Cornelis de Bruijn in Java.
1756	Final Dutch voyage to Australia, by Gonzal and van Aaschens, explores eastern Arnhemland and the Gulf of Carpentaria.
1768–1771	First voyage of James Cook, landing on Australia's east coast, New Zealand, Tahiti. With this voyage the notion of a Great Southland is finally dispelled.

Preface

The central thesis of this book was formulated in 1986–88, during the intensive planning stages of the Australian Bicentennial exhibition 'Terra Australis', which I curated for the Art Gallery of New South Wales. Of the many Australian friends who assisted me during those trying but exhilarating days, I should give particular thanks to Professor Bernard Smith, whose fundamental studies inspired my own efforts, Professor Virginia Spate, Power Professor of Contemporary Art at the University of Sydney, who encouraged me to take up the challenge, and Mr Barry Pearce, Curator of Australian Art at the AGNSW, who supported the exhibition project from beginning to end. A Research Fellowship at the John Carter Brown Library at Brown University (Summer 1989) enabled me to refine my ideas in a congenial and stimulating environment, encouraged and assisted by the Library's Director, Dr Norman Fiering.

I am especially grateful to Dr Robin Derricourt of Cambridge University Press for offering me the opportunity to publish the present work, to Ms Phillipa McGuinness of the Editorial Department at CUP for supervising the preparation of the text and the procurement of the illustrations, and to Mr Roderic Campbell for his diligent and skilful efforts as editor. Above all I am indebted to my wife Dominique, who supported me during the entire period of the writing of the text, and to two extraordinary boys, Yvan and Leonel.

William Eisler
St-Saphorin, Switzerland

Introduction

1

The Americas loomed ever larger in the European imagination over the centuries but, by contrast, the gradual unveiling of the mist surrounding the southern continent produced an inverse effect. The image of a vast, imaginary Terra Australis, widely disseminated during the sixteenth century, eventually dissolved into Australia, New Guinea, Antarctica, the South Pacific islands, and Tierra del Fuego.

The iconography of the southern world – the subject of this book – can therefore be reconstructed only as an assemblage of fragments, linked together in the mind. These elements were derived from a long series of European voyages in both the eastern and western hemispheres and therefore relate to the discovery of both Asia and America. Their evolution was affected by innovations in the depiction of nature and human types, as well as by the ideological concerns of the great maritime powers. Furthermore, this imagery did not 'develop'; nor was it received in a uniform manner by an undifferentiated 'European public'. Images – painted, drawn and engraved, published and unpublished, altered and transformed – were created for and examined by a highly stratified and complex European society.[1]

This volume discusses visual imagery associated with Terra Australis from the Middle Ages to the first voyage of Captain James Cook (1768–71). Emphasis has been placed upon pictorial works – drawings, paintings, and engravings. However, a number of maps have also been included, especially those which are illuminated with depictions of coastlines, animals, plants, native people, and so on. As this is not a history of the discovery of Australia or the Pacific, it has not been necessary to include every important map and chart relevant to those themes. Nevertheless, I have incorporated cartographic documents essential for placing the pictorial imagery in its geographical and historical context.

The imagery associated with the search for Terra Australis discussed in this work has in turn been evaluated in terms of the entire history of art and exploration. Scholars have generally considered the history of exploration in relationship to a single geographic area: the Americas, Asia, or the Pacific. As a result the sense of a European presence simultaneously in all parts of the world has been lost. By providing a wider base for comparative study, the phenomena can be studied with greater profit.

Over time the pictures from a southern world evoked what was essentially a bipolar vision of Terra Australis prior to the great Pacific voyages of the late eighteenth century: on the one hand, that of a generally barren region inhabited by brute savages; on the other, a more beautiful, plentiful land with a far more attractive and hospitable population. In the wake of Cook's voyages (1768–80) this dichotomy would be transformed into two parallel visions: that of a desolate world of 'hard' primitives (Fuegans, Maoris, Papuans and Australian Aborigines) and a paradise of 'soft' primitives (Tahitians and other South Pacific islanders).

Readers familiar with the subject will recognize a link between my conclusions and certain observations in Bernard Smith's fundamental study, *European Vision and the South Pacific 1768–1850. A Study in the History of Art and Ideas* (Oxford 1960, reprinted Sydney 1985 without significant change but with a new introduction by the author):

The first European visitors to Polynesia tended to view the natives as noble savages, an attitude with its roots deep in the thought of classical antiquity. It is possible to distinguish two forms of this primitivistic

approach to Pacific peoples: a soft primitivism, applied mainly to the
inhabitants of the Society Islands, and a hard primitivism, applied to
such peoples as the Fuegans, the Maoris, and the Australian aborigines.[2]

Smith argues that these classical notions of soft and hard primitivism were
gradually eliminated by more objective, scientific research in the Pacific,
facilitated by a new form of objective visual representation. The confrontation
between the classicizing and scientific mentalities is said to have occurred in
the second half of the eighteenth century as a consequence of the great
Pacific voyages of Cook (1768–80). The long history of art and exploration is
therefore not discussed, nor is the European presence in the Pacific for two
centuries prior to Cook's voyages.[3]

Smith's account begins from a time when certain elements of Pacific
geography were already known. The essential elements of the myth of a
Pacific paradise, and its antithesis, the infernal Southland, existed at the
beginning of the eighteenth century. The formulation of these two visions was
in fact facilitated by the same 'scientific' means of graphic representation
which, in Smith's view, contributed to their gradual disappearance.

The premises of *European Vision and the South Pacific* are therefore
very different from those of the present work, although I have profited greatly
from the immense scholarly efforts of its author. Before proceeding further, it
is useful to summarize the essential aspects of this exceedingly influential
volume.

Seeking to describe the early development of European painting in
Australia, Smith traces its origins to the voyage of Captain James Cook and
Joseph Banks to the Pacific (1768–71), designated by the author as the first
large-scale scientific expedition in which art played a major role. The voyage
was sponsored by the Royal Society and its investigations of flora and fauna
were inspired by Enlightenment science, notably the classification system of
Linnaeus. The consequent development in Australia of what is described as
the typical landscape, revealing the specific qualities of a place, is viewed as
the outgrowth of the precise studies made by expedition artists from the time
of Cook to the middle of the nineteenth century. Careful observations of
Pacific topography, natural phenomena, and human types produced by artists
working in collaboration with scientists, contributed to the development of a
new landscape genre.

The significance of this innovation had repercussions beyond the limits
of the history of art:

> The idea of the typical in landscape-painting parallels in point of time
> the emergence of the idea of organic evolution in science. It will be
> shown that in the Pacific these two matters were closely connected. In
> both is to be witnessed the abandonment of classical ideals of order, for
> an order based upon a closer scrutiny of things in themselves. In its
> mature forms, the typical landscape provides an artistic counterpart to
> the biological explanation of life upon the planet provided by the theory
> of organic evolution.[4]

In the introductory chapter the author emphasizes the coincidence in date between Cook's first voyage – sponsored by the Royal Society – and the founding of the Royal Academy as a bastion of neoclassical taste. The empirical studies promoted by the Royal Society enabled Europeans to comprehend the reality of the new world of the Pacific, its people, flora, and fauna, thereby destroying the classicizing myth of an Arcadian island realm, created by the academicians and their supporters. Smith notes that since Elizabethan times navigators had been instructed to make careful observations and to keep diaries; however, the process was greatly enhanced by the Society's inclusion of artists on Cook's voyages. Their studies would contribute to profound changes in Western notions regarding the origin of life:

> As scientists came to question the teleological position implicit in the view of nature as a great chain of being, they tended to seek an explanation for the origin and nature of life in the material evidence provided by the earth's surface. The intense study of rocks, plants, animals, people, and the laws governing climatic conditions acquired a new significance even for the landscape-painter. For such things held the clue to the meaning of nature and the origin of life. It was most desirable, therefore, that the artist should depict them accurately, for it was only by the closest scrutiny and the most careful description that they could be made to yield their meaning.[5]

The artist's ability to render the myriad, hitherto unknown forms of life and matter in an objective manner complemented the work of Charles Darwin, Joseph Dalton Hooker, and Thomas Henry Huxley, all of whom studied the natural history of the Pacific. Their investigations in this vast and strange realm served as evidence for a new theory of evolution based upon natural selection.[6] Both the vision of a Pacific paradise, based upon neoclassical Arcadian imagery, and its inverse, the evil world of wanton savages portrayed in missionary tracts, were swept aside by the new science and art: 'In the end scientific method triumphed in the description both of nature and man'.[7]

Scientific progress was therefore paralleled – and assisted – by progress in the arts. According to Smith's thesis, a line might be drawn linking the artists who accompanied Cook to the founders of landscape painting in the Australian colonies. The work of Sydney Parkinson, William Hodges, and John Webber on Cook's voyages initiated a process which culminated in the Australian views of Darwin's shipmate Conrad Martens, draughtsman on the *Beagle*.[8] The atmospheric naturalism of Hodges's Pacific images constitutes the first stage in a development leading to the Australian landscapes of Martens, which – however romantic they may appear – are in essence faithful renderings of natural forms.

In the light of research conducted over the past three decades, Bernard Smith's integration of the histories of scientific and ethnographic illustration, evolutionary thought, and Australian art in one vast progression appears somewhat forced. I prefer to see these strands as running parallel to each other, intersecting at various points. The year 1768 marks an important stage in this history. Rather than viewing it as a point of departure we may also consider it as a final episode, the moment in which the ancient vision of Terra Australis ceased to exist.

Professor Smith's argument is based upon an association of certain intellectual constructs and historical phenomena. We must question whether they are as tightly woven together as he suggests. Let us consider for example the terms 'Australia', and 'the South Pacific'. Much of Australia in reality is closer to Indonesia and New Guinea than to Tahiti, the focus of Cook's first voyage (and of the first part of *European Vision*). This is an important point; for, prior to Cook, the continent was inevitably compared with Asia and the East Indies. Most geographers believed that it shared a coastline with New Guinea, and this hypothetical connection appeared to be confirmed by the presence of similar flora and fauna and equally 'savage' inhabitants in both regions. Dutch expeditions to Australia in the seventeenth and eighteenth centuries were undertaken in the vain hope that Australia/New Guinea might be absorbed into their East Indian domain, rich in spices and other natural products. Indeed, during the first years of its existence, the survival of the British colony in New South Wales depended upon supplies and food from the territories controlled by the Dutch East India Company.[9] Therefore, a discussion centred upon European images of Australia and Polynesia under the general rubric of the South Pacific is somewhat misleading. Australia and its Aborigines were judged principally against the yardstick of Asia, the East Indies, New Guinea, and their inhabitants.

It may be argued, however, that the main purpose of *European Vision* was to describe the manner in which a supposedly objective art form, employed on the first great scientific voyages (beginning with Cook) helped to create the 'typical' landscape, the antithesis of the neoclassical. In the process, a new, more modern artistic vision, recording the wonders of a previously unknown Australian/Pacific world, contributed to the development of a more advanced explanation for the origins and transformations of living beings – Darwin's theory of evolution.

My research has led to a different conclusion. The phenomena described by Bernard Smith – the association of art, science, exploration, and the 'typical' landscape – had made their appearance at a much earlier date. They were products of the Renaissance, not the Enlightenment. The roots of these phenomena can be traced to the early sixteenth century, the age of Raphael and his followers, whose works served as models for the neo-classicists. Their role in the history of Western visual culture during the Early Modern period was as significant as the revival of interest in classical form.

The efforts of artists and scientists to describe and depict hitherto unknown species and human types were undertaken on a global scale well before the time of Cook. In the pages that follow we will examine the images they produced, the audiences for which they were intended, and their complex relationship to the changing vision of the southern world.

A brief note on terminology before proceeding. The reader may be confused by the variety of terms employed to describe the main subject of this essay. The apparent lack of precision on my part is unavoidable, as the actual geographical configuration of the southern hemisphere was not fully known until the nineteenth century. 'Antipodes' refers both to the medieval monsters with reversed feet and the southern region in which they supposedly dwelled; in each case the exact meaning should be clear from the context. 'Terra Australis' was the descriptive term applied to the continent thought to fill the entire southern portion of the globe. In the latter half of the sixteenth century 'Magellanica' came into use to refer to the same region. Both of these designations were employed in the sixteenth, seventeenth, and eighteenth centuries. However, from the early seventeenth century to the late eighteenth century the terms 'Southland' or 'Great Southland' were applied to Spanish and Dutch discoveries in Australia, New Guinea, and New Zealand, as well as Melanesia and western Polynesia. 'New Holland' refers exclusively to the mainland of Australia. Regrettably, it is not possible to be more specific regarding the boundaries of these vaguely known, partly imaginary lands.

All translations from foreign languages are my own, unless otherwise noted.

Part

The Invention of a

Southern Continent

I

Terra Australis

in Antiquity

and the Middle Ages

2

Prior to the Renaissance the austral continent was a pure abstraction, as few in the West had travelled to the southern hemisphere.[1] Belief in its existence, a point of intense discussion in antiquity, was judged as heretical during the Middle Ages. The presence of its image on medieval *mappae mundi*, therefore, attests to the persistence of Greco-Roman geographical theory in the scholastic world.

The invention of the concept of a southern continent is generally credited to Pythagoras. He divided the world into five parts: two frigid and temperate zones located north and south of a torrid equator. In the geographical treatise of Crates of Mallos (second century BC) the earth's surface consisted of four landmasses: two in the northern hemisphere and two in the southern. These were separated from each other by two great oceans, one encircling the earth at the equator, the other dividing the planet on the north/south axis. Although Crates believed that each zone was completely inaccessible from the other, he allowed for the possibility of an inhabited southern world. Pomponius Mela (*De Situ Orbis*, first century AD), likewise postulated the existence of a great austral continent, separated from his own by a vast equatorial ocean; Ceylon was thought to be a promontory of this distant world. Ptolemey, the greatest of all ancient geographers, believed that a *terra incognita* (unknown land) formed the southern enclosure of the Atlantic and Indian oceans.

During the Middle Ages, speculation concerning a southern continent and its inhabitants was generally, although not consistently, opposed by Christian dogma. St Augustine (354–430) declared the southern portion of the earthly sphere to be entirely ocean. He rejected the notion of a race of men with feet opposed to our own, or antipodes (figure 1) inhabiting the other side of the earth. The entire theory was considered heretical, as it presupposed the

1 Hartmann Schedel, *Antipode*, 1493, woodcut from *Liber Chronicarum (Nuremberg Chronicle)*, Mitchell Library, State Library of New South Wales

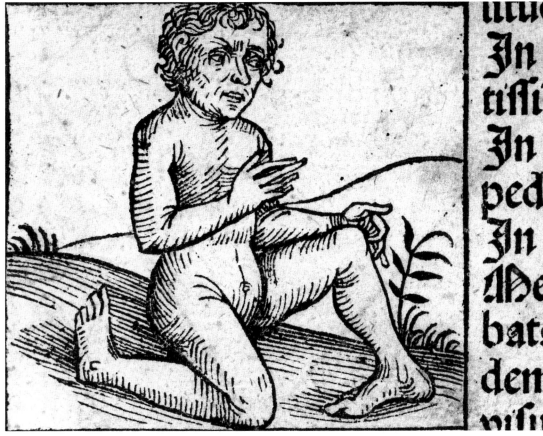

creation of a separate race of men who would remain ignorant of the Gospel. Isidore of Seville (ca. 560–636) in his encyclopedic *Etymologies* preferred to leave the question open, referring to an extremely hot, inaccessible fourth landmass, the place where the antipodes (erroneously in his view) were alleged to live. In a separate section of his text, however, he locates this fabulous race in the Libyan desert.

If Isidore seems to have harboured some doubts on the question, the followers of Macrobius were more certain. In his commentary on Cicero's *Republic*, the *Dream of Scipio* (fifth century AD), a summary of Neoplatonic astronomy and geography, Macrobius describes a five-part world, comparable to that of Pythagoras, consisting of a 'frigida septemtrionalis inhabitabilis', a 'temperata habitabilis', a 'perusta inhabitabilis', a 'temperata habitabilis (antipodium)', and a 'frigida australis inhabitabilis'. Although the temperate portion of the southern hemisphere may well be inhabited by an antipodean race, the torrid central zone would render it inaccessible to the rest of the world.

Manuscripts of the *Dream of Scipio* executed between the ninth and the fifteenth centuries include maps illustrating Macrobius's geographical concept. The influence of his thought may also be perceived in other medieval works, notably the circular *mappa mundi* contained in the *Liber Floridus* of Lambert de Saint-Omer (twelfth century). In this instance the zone devoted to Terra Australis is nearly equal to that of Europe, Asia, and Africa. An extended caption describes the land as 'unknown to the descendants of Adam', inhabited by a race having nothing in common with our own.

Other types of medieval maps upon which the Terra Australis is clearly configured are the Beatus world maps or *mappae mundi*. Tripartite and oval in form, they allot a narrow strip in the southern zone to an austral region. The maps illustrate the commentary to the Apocalypse of St John by the Asturian monk Beatus of Liébana (eighth century), specifically the section devoted to the evangelization of the world by the Twelve Apostles. The caption to the representation of the fourth part of the world cites Isidore of Seville's remarks concerning the fabled existence of the antipodes. In the so-called *Osma Beatus* (1086) a skiapod, one of the more commonly depicted medieval monsters, is shown in this region, shielding himself from the blazing sun with his enormous single foot (figure 2).[2]

The *mappa mundi* in the *Osma Beatus* is an important visual document in the iconography of Terra Australis, for now this hypothetical land is depicted as a populated region. Actually, the presence of the skiapod cannot be justified by the citation from Isidore, who denied the possibility of a habitable austral continent. Its residents in any event were alleged to be antipodes, not skiapodes. The latter's presence is the earliest example of the imaginative displacements which pervade the iconography of Terra Australis.

In the course of the twelfth and thirteenth centuries a revived interest in the science and philosophy of the ancients, notably the works of Ptolemey and Aristotle, encouraged renewed speculation regarding Terra Australis. One of the principal proponents of the concept was Albertus Magnus (1206–80),

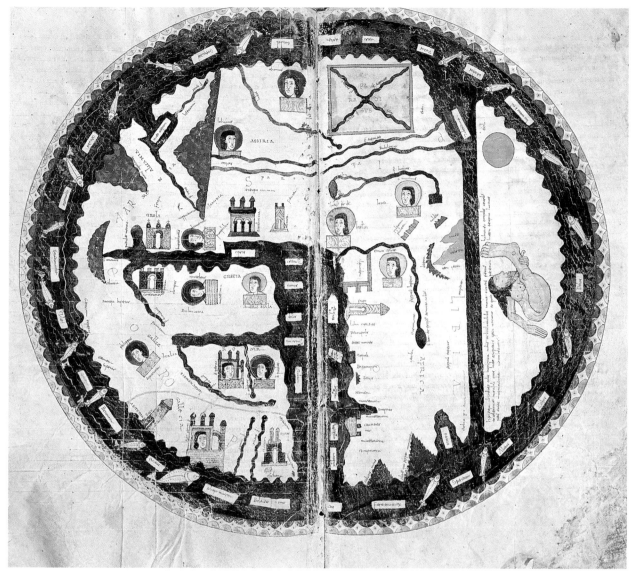

2 *Mappa mundi (World Map)*, 11th century, MS., *Osma Beatus*, Cathedral, Burgo de Osma (reproduced in colour following page 44)

teacher of Thomas Aquinas, who argued that humans would thrive in the temperate zones between the 24th and 48th parallels north and south of the equator. Towards the end of this period the travel accounts of Marco Polo (1254–1324) incorporated descriptions of thriving civilizations in the supposedly uninhabitable torrid zones. These reports passed into legend, merging with other accounts of the marvels of the east. By the mid-sixteenth century, Marco Polo's accounts of the wealth of the Indies had become identified in the European imagination with certain unknown but purportedly rich kingdoms lying to the south and east of Indonesia mentioned in the Venetian traveller's text: Beach, Lucach, and Maletur – legendary realms which on the maps of the period would occupy the space corresponding to Western Australia. Gerard Mercator, for instance, incorporated the three kingdoms Marco Polo described into Terra Australis on his 1541 world map (see chapter 3).

Terra Australis
in the Early Renaissance

3

In the second half of the fifteenth century the revival of antique geography provided a more authoritative basis for the belief in a landmass lying south of the known world. In a splendid hand-coloured version of Ptolemey's *Geographia* published in Ulm (1482), the *terra incognita* is conjoined with Africa in the west and the Asian continent to the east, forming the southern shore of the Indian Ocean (figure 3). Printed editions of the *Dream of Scipio* (Venice 1472) and *De Situ Orbis* (Venice 1482) further stimulated the imagination.

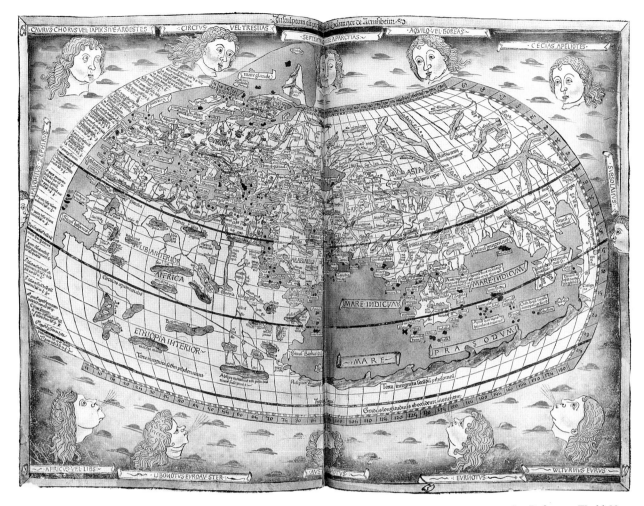

3 Ptolemey, *World Map*, 1482, woodcut from *Geographia*, by permission of the British Library

In the course of the fifteenth century, Portuguese navigators began to penetrate into the southern regions of the world, which hitherto had been merely the subject of speculation. Sailing along the West African coast, by 1470 they had crossed the equator, in the process dispelling the myth of an uninhabitable torrid zone. The Portuguese explorers expressed little interest in speculations regarding Terra Australis, preferring to concentrate on exploiting the riches of the Indies. However, the precise methods of graphic observation developed on their naval expeditions would contribute to the visual documentation of the southern world.

The third voyage of Amerigo Vespucci (1454–1512), on behalf of the Portuguese crown, opens a new chapter in the history of the image of Terra Australis. The purpose of the expedition (1501–02) was to inspect the newly discovered Tierra de Santa Cruz (Brazil) and to seek a westward passage further south. Vespucci led a fleet of Portuguese vessels along the southern coast of South America, reaching the River Plate and Patagonia. In the process he came to the momentous conclusion that he had, in fact, discovered a new antipodean continent. In the text of his letter to Lorenzo di

Pierfrancesco de' Medici announcing his discovery (first published as *Mundus Novus* ca. 1503), a work of enormous impact, Vespucci paints a glowing picture of the land and its inhabitants:

4 Oronce Finé, *Nova, et integro universi Orbis Descriptio*, 1531, woodcut, by permission of the British Library

I found myself in the region of the Antipodes … This land is very
agreeable, full of tall trees which never lose their leaves and give off
the sweetest odors … Often I believed myself to be in Paradise …

What can one say regarding the quantity of animals in the forests ... I
believe that there had been more species than those which disembarked
from the Ark ... This land is populated by people who are entirely
nude, both men and women ... They have no law, nor any religion, they
live according to nature and without any knowledge of the immortality
of the soul. They have no private property, everything is owned
communally; they have no borders between provinces and countries,
they have no king and are subject to no one.[1]

In Vespucci's mind Paradise and Utopia merged in the splendours of an
antipodean world; brilliantly coloured parrots from these newly discovered
southern regions decorate the earliest cartographic representations of Brazil
(for instance, the Cantino map of 1502).[2] During the initial decades of the
sixteenth century, however, there was great confusion as to where Vespucci's
discoveries should be located cartographically. On the first globe by Johann
Schöner (1515) a vast 'Brasilia Regio' is represented, separated from South
America by a channel. In a later version (1520) it is designated as 'Brasilia
Inferior' and clearly distinguished from Brazil proper, or 'Papagalli Terra'. In
Oronce Finé's map of the world (1531) 'Brasilia Regio' lies to the southeast of
Madagascar, depicted as a peninsula of a massive Terra Australis (figure 4).
A decade later, Vespucci's land of parrots ('Psittacorum Regio'), completely
detached from its South American context, would be incorporated into Gerard
Mercator's great austral continent, directly south of the Cape of Good Hope
(see figure 15).

5 Francisco Rodrigues,
Livro, 1512, MS.,
Bibliothèque de
l'Assemblée Nationale,
Paris

The Portuguese approach

Terra Australis from the East

While Vespucci was exploring what he believed to be the antipodes in the western hemisphere, Portuguese navigators sailed in the direction of the actual Australian continent from the east. By 1488 they had circled the Cape of Good Hope, arriving on the coast of India ten years later. In 1511 they had established a trading base at Malacca, on the Malay peninsula, and the following year the expedition of Francisco Rodrigues had arrived in Banda, approximately 900 kilometres from present-day Darwin, Northern Territory. The Portuguese were not preoccupied with the search for a southern continent. Whether or not they reached Australia in the early sixteenth century, as some authorities believe, cannot be determined; in any case their maps and charts do not record a discovery of this nature. What is certain is that in the course of their explorations in eastern waters they devised extra-ordinary pictorial records of seas and shorelines, plants, animals, and even meteorological phenomena, more than two and a half centuries before Cook.

One of the most important forms of graphic documentation employed by Portuguese explorers was the rutter, a collection of coastal views, constituting 'an accepted type of maritime record dating back to the fifteenth century'.[3] A remarkable example is a manuscript by Francisco Rodrigues in the Bibliothèque de l'Assemblée Nationale, Paris, incorporating a set of pen

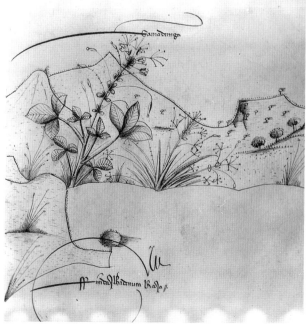

drawings produced in the course of his return voyage from Banda to Malacca in 1512 (figure 5). When joined together, the views provide a nearly continuous profile of the north coasts of the chain of islands from Alor to western Java. These vigorously executed panoramic drawings, replete with vivid details of topography, native habitations, mosques, and vegetation, are perhaps the earliest images of the tropical islands lying to the northwest of the Australian continent.[4] The intense concentration of diverse elements within each sheet contrasts with the more sober, detached, 'scientific' views executed by Cook's artists.

In the course of their oceanic voyages, Portuguese navigators, like their eighteenth-century British counterparts, were struck by the power of natural forces, both threatening and enthralling. In a rutter describing his voyage from Lisbon to Goa, the viceroy of the Portuguese Indies João de Castro incorporated a detailed description of a waterspout observed on 14 July 1538, accompanied by his own drawing (figure 6).[5] The text and illustration may well have inspired a vivid passage in *The Lusiads*, the epic poem by the viceroy's friend Luiz de Camões:

6 João de Castro, *Waterspout*, 1538, pen drawing from his *Roteiro from Lisbon to Goa*, MS., Biblioteca Pública, Évora

I do not think that my sight cheated me,
For certainly I saw rise up in the air
A smoke of fine and vaporous subtility,
That whirled perpetual, as the wind might bear.
To the high pole rose the spout, as one might see,
And yet was so tenuous and rare,
Discovery by the eye was scarce allowed.
It seemed the very substance of a cloud.
Little by little waxing the thing grew
Till it was thicker than the mightiest mast.
Here it might thin or thicken out anew,
As it sucked up the sea with gulpings vast.
Within the rolling wave it undulated too.
On its head a dense cloud darkened, overcast.
That swelled apace and still more ponderous showed,
For water it took up, a monstrous load. (V, 19–20)[6]

Comparable emotions of fascination and awe were undoubtedly felt by the artist William Hodges and the scientists aboard Cook's vessel the *Resolution* on 17 May 1773, when four waterspouts were observed off Cape Stephens, New Zealand. Hodges prepared sketches, which served as the basis of an engraving illustrating the published account of the incident. The waterspouts also inspired one of the artist's most impressive works, the 'View of Cape Stephens' (figure 7), which, as Bernard Smith has noted, parallels a written description by George Forster. Consciously or not, the works of Hodges and Forster off the New Zealand coast were executed in the spirit of a long tradition in visual and literary culture.[7]

Portuguese interest in natural phenomena was paralleled elsewhere in Europe; Leonardo's drawings of plants, animals, and cataclysmic storms come immediately to mind. In Germany the drawings and engravings of Albrecht Dürer inspired an autonomous genre of scientific illustration. In the watercolours of Hans Weiditz and Conrad Gessner plants are rendered so as to reveal their structure, to provide identifiable models for botanists and physicians. However beautiful they may appear, they were not intended as works of art in themselves nor as preliminary studies for paintings.[8] With the increase in the quantity of known species and the intensification of the search for new medicines, botanical illustration became more closely affiliated with science and exploration. Likewise, the studies of animals and birds by Leonardo and Dürer inspired an extensive illustrated zoological literature in the sixteenth century, incorporating pictures and descriptions of species from abroad. These volumes reflected not only an increased scientific interest, but also a fascination with the rare and exotic.

The study of what we may term ethnographic illustration also developed during the first quarter of the sixteenth century. An increased interest in rendering what was distinctive and different in terms of dress and appearance –

7 William Hodges,
*A View of Cape Stephens
in Cook's Straits (New
Zealand) with
Waterspouts,* 1776, oil on
canvas, National Maritime
Museum, London

exemplified by such works as Dürer's drawings of Irish soldiers and peasants,
or his sensitive portrait of an African servant girl – coincided with the period
of Portuguese exploration during the initial decades of the sixteenth century.[9]
A remarkable work from this period is a woodcut series by Hans Burgkmair,
illustrating the account of a voyage of Balthasar Springer, an Augsburg
merchant, to India in 1505–06. The series consists of a frieze-like arrange-
ment of figures depicting natives of Africa and India, derived from first-hand
sketches. Although the figural types are considerably idealized, the artist has
made a concerted effort to capture distinctive dress, weapons and other
paraphernalia of these inhabitants of the southern world. We may imagine
that Burgkmair's family of Hottentots, or his procession of the king of Cochin
(figure 8) in the same series must have produced a strong effect on the
spectator, more accustomed to representations of Roman triumphs in the
manner of Mantegna.[10] And Dürer himself produced one of the finest of these
rare early images of foreign exotica: a drawing of a Tupinimba Indian from
Portuguese Brazil, resplendent in his feather skirt and head-dress.[11] The
care with which the artist has rendered these exotic elements reflects his
documented interest in the art of the Americas.[12]

In the course of the third decade of the sixteenth century, Amerigo
Vespucci's image of an antipodean paradise would be supplanted by a less

8 Hans Burgkmair, *The King of Cochin*, ca. 1508, woodcut, by permission of the British Library

idyllic vision of the antipodes in the western hemisphere: the cold southern extremities of America, discovered by Magellan in the course of his global journey. The location of this portion of Terra Australis would be fixed to the south of the Strait of Magellan, the newly found passage linking the Atlantic and Pacific oceans traversed by the Portuguese explorer in the course of the voyage. Fires lit by natives on the shoreline observed in the course of the voyage would inspire the name of this desolate region: Tierra del Fuego.

Java la Grande

and Magellanica

4

The circumnavigation of the globe undertaken by Ferdinand Magellan on behalf of the Holy Roman Emperor Charles V (1519–22) produced a radically new cartographic image of the world. Only three of the original five ships remained when the Portuguese navigator crossed the dangerous straits and entered the Pacific. Sailing northwest, he discovered Guam after one hundred days in the vast ocean; soon afterwards he reached the Philippines, entering into an alliance with the king of Cebu. After the commander's death at the hands of Philippine warriors, the vessels set sail for the Moluccas; only one, however, the *Victoria*, with a crew of eighteen, reached Seville in September 1522.

No drawings of the regions explored by Magellan and his expedition survive. The images accompanying the most authoritative manuscript version of Antonio Pigafetta's account of the voyage (in the Beinicke Library, Yale University) are completely in the style of the late Middle Ages – for example, the charming depiction of an outrigger canoe from the Marianas. The text itself is a mélange of careful observation (including American Indian and Indonesian vocabularies) and fantastic accounts of Patagonian giants.[1]

Within a few years a new and more complex image of Terra Australis would make its appearance:

> Although while in the Straits Magellan's people had thought that they could hear the surge on a distant shore to the south, and had correctly deduced that the land to their left was insular, yet, as T. H. Parry points out, Tierra del Fuego 'gained a new lease of cartographical life' for Terra Australis, the temptation to carry it on across the Mar del Sur proving irresistible to generations of cosmographers. Yet even this was a spur to new explorations. No other single voyage has ever added so much to the dimension of the world.[2]

Even though the idea of an extensive southern continent was by no means universally accepted, most sixteenth century maps represented Tierra del Fuego as part of a larger landmass located to the south of the Americas. This zone would constitute the point of departure for a multitude of cartographic images of a fifth continent. One of the most intriguing of these configurations took form in France around 1540: the enigmatic region known as Java la Grande. Inspired by rumours and reports of Portuguese explorations to the east of Indonesia, this territory appeared on a series of important French maps executed over a period of approximately twenty-five years. Its disappearance from European world maps coincided with the emergence of a more extensive southern continent, Magellanica – a configuration which would dominate European geographic thought well into the seventeenth century.

Java la Grande:
French Imagery of the
Unknown World ca. 1540–66

As it appears on the maps of the Dieppe cartographers, Java la Grande is a landmass bearing a certain superficial resemblance to Australia, and lying to the southeast of Sumatra. The apparent similarity has inspired some historians to argue that the configuration derives from the Portuguese discovery of the fifth continent. Whether or not this is the case, it is undeniable that the Dieppe cartographers believed that Java la Grande was indeed the southern continent (or *a* southern continent, or possibly a promontory of Terra Australis, like Tierra del Fuego). In any case its importance for the history of images of the antipodes is unquestionable.

9 Jean Rotz, *World Map*, 1542, MS., from his *Boke of Idrography*, by permission of the British Library

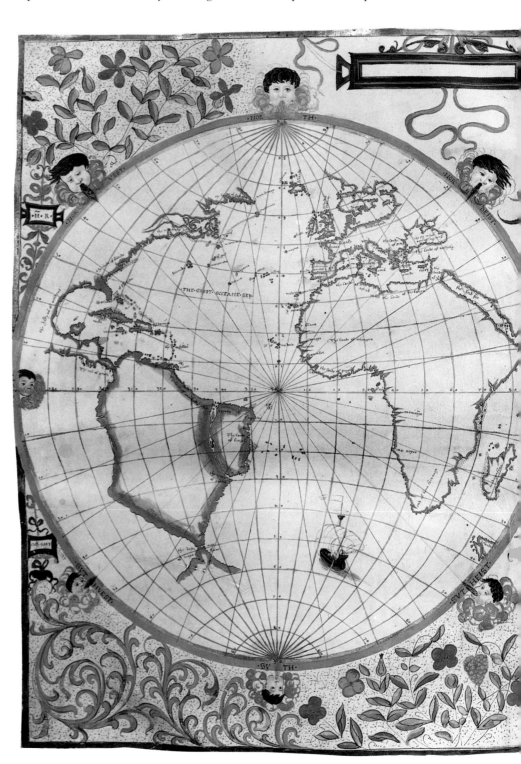

Helen Wallis, a principal authority on the theories concerning Java la Grande and Renaissance cartography in general, has observed that:

> Dieppe was the great centre of French maritime activity, with *armateurs* (ship fitters-out) who acted independently of the cautious king and his government in Paris. [The historian] Charles la Ronçière has

commented: 'If you are looking for the dominant force in maritime politics in France, don't go to the court of Francis I but to Dieppe.'[3]

The coastal city, therefore, represented an alternative centre of thought and action within the state. In terms of the figurative arts, as well, it remained distinct from the royal court, as we shall see. The *armateurs* of Dieppe wished to challenge the Portuguese monopoly on the East Indies trade, granted to Lisbon as a consequence of the treaty of Tordesillas in 1494. In the process they perfected their rivals' techniques in the representation of distant lands.

In 1529 the most ambitious of these Dieppe *armateurs*, Jean Ango, launched an expedition towards the furthest extremities of the Portuguese eastern realm. On 31 October the explorer Jean Parmentier, accompanied by his brother Raoul, and the navigator Pierre Crignon, arrived in Sumatra. There, the two brothers died of fever. During the course of their visit to the island they learned of the arrival of two white men the previous year, sent by a great king. After voting to decide whether to continue on to 'Java', they resolved to return home. Crignon brought the ships back to France via the Cape of Good Hope, arriving in Europe in the summer of 1530.[4]

On the basis of this account it is difficult to concur with the views of certain scholars that the survivors of the Parmentier expedition had definite knowledge of a Portuguese discovery of Australia. What is certain is that within the circle of the Dieppe cartographers the belief existed that a continent called Java constituted Terra Australis or at least a part of it. The first written report of this region was prepared by Jean Alphonse, a Portuguese pilot living in France. In a manuscript of ca. 1536 (most likely an early version of his *Voyages avantureux*, Poitiers, 1559) he describes 'la terre de Jave' as a land south of Sumatra inhabited by a people similar to those of Brazil, rich in gold, with splendid rivers. Conflating his account with those of Marco Polo, he notes that the people of Java worship the sun and moon. The sea between Sumatra and 'la terre de Jave' was so dangerous that ships could not pass across. Alphonse's image of Javanese devotees would appear in the form of vignettes on maps of the Dieppe school, as would his 'dangerous coasts'.[5] In the text of his *Cosmographie* (1544), composed of seventy manuscript maps, he describes 'la grande Java' as:

> a land which extends down near to the Antarctic pole; on the western side it is close to the Southern Land, and on the eastern side to the Strait of Magellan. Some say that it is made up of islands. But as regards what I have seen of it, it is a continent ... The land called Java Minor is an island. But Great Java is a continent ...[6]

Although he did not belong to the Dieppe school, Alphonse had access to charts and documents from this great maritime centre. His description of Java la Grande corresponds with representations of the region by Dieppe cartographers. In some maps and charts (for example, the world maps of

Pierre Desceliers of 1546, 1550, and 1553) it is directly linked to Tierra del Fuego. In other examples (the *Rotz Atlas* of 1542, the *Harleian World Map* of ca. 1547) the connection is less explicit, as both areas run off the map at the southern edge. In any case it is certain that Java la Grande was thought to be *a* Terre Australe, if not part of *the* Terre Australe.

The earliest major cartographic work depicting the land of Java is also one of the finest works of art of the French Renaissance. The *Boke of Idrography* (1542), more commonly known as the *Rotz Atlas*, consists of eleven regional charts and a double-page map of the world.[7] This splendid work was begun in France by the cartographer and artist Jean Rotz as a presentation work for King Francis I. It was completed on behalf of the English king, Henry VIII, after its author crossed the Channel in search of a more favourable court position. A massive continental Java la Grande is depicted on the world map (figure 9) while its northern boundary appears on the chart representing Sumatra (figure 10).

10 Jean Rotz, *Chart of Southeast Asia*, 1542, MS., from his *Boke of Idrography*, by permission of the British Library (reproduced in colour following page 44)

The *Rotz Atlas* provides an encyclopedic record of voyages directed by Jean Ango. The regional charts, based upon the latest cartographic evidence,

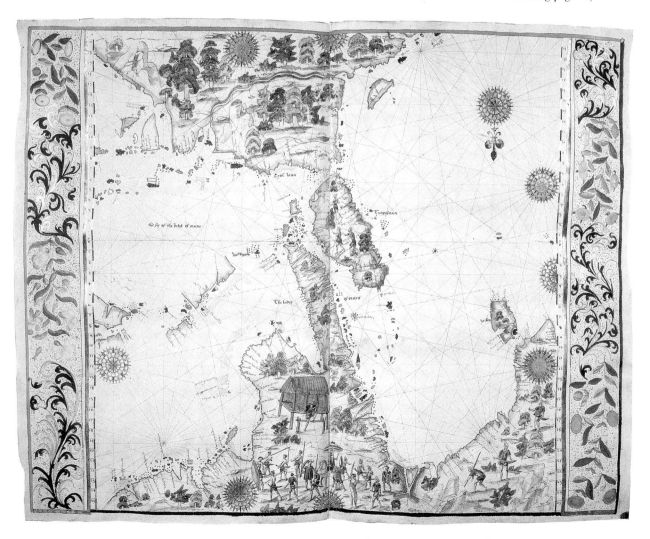

are illustrated with detailed vignettes of non-European cultures in the
eastern and western hemisphere, many of which are clearly based on direct
observations by expedition artists. Rotz's volume is much more than an atlas
of the world; it is an innovatory work reflecting a new mentality in visual

11 *Java la Grande*,
1547, MS., from the
Vallard Atlas, by
permission of The
Huntington Library, San
Marino, California

representation. At the same time, its full meaning could only be appreciated within the immediate circle of its royal patron. The special qualities of Rotz's handiwork are precisely summarized in the author's dedication to the king:

For in this work, Sire, after labouring for the affairs and public good of
your most excellent Kingdom and people, you may for the recreation of
your noble mind observe and learn which coastal lands adjoin or face
one another, how many leagues apart they are and in what latitude,
together with the style and manner of the houses, clothes and skin
colour, as well as arms and other features of all the coasts which are
least known to us.[8]

The veracity of this claim is made evident throughout the manuscript. Among
the finest of Rotz's images is a precise rendering of a Tupinimba stockaded
village in Brazil, probably derived from drawings executed by the cartographer himself in the course of a voyage to South America in 1539.[9] A
number of the vignettes, including those representing the inhabitants of
Sumatra, the Hottentots at the Cape of Good Hope, and a violent encounter
in Madagascar, are closely related to the written account of the Parmentier
expedition. These pictures are most likely the work of Jean Sasi, 'dit le Grand
Peintre', who accompanied the French explorers. Especially noteworthy is the
vignette illustrating the map of southeast Asia, which closely follows the
textual description of Ticou, western Sumatra. The procession of the rajah of
Ticou is replete with explicit details of costume and weaponry. A
characteristic Sumatran pile-dwelling with an exterior stoop (the wooden
cross-beam erected in front of the building and intended to facilitate entrance
to the building) likewise corresponds to the written description. The
specificity of this image is particularly apparent when compared to a later
version in the *Vallard Atlas*, another masterpiece of Dieppe cartography. Here
the stoop device is completely misunderstood by the artist, who places it at a
considerable distance from the entrance to the house (figure 11).[10]

The extraordinarily specific images in the *Rotz Atlas*, rendering what is
particular to hitherto unknown cultures, were created in an intellectual and
social environment which was distinct from the one that produced the
contemporaneous Mannerist decorations in the château of Fontainebleau by
Rosso and Primaticcio, with their studied rhetoric and elegant pathos. The
sketches and drawings employed by Rotz represent a highly sophisticated
form of research, intended in the first instance as visual aids for navigators,
explorers and their sponsors. At a later stage his works were transformed into
illustrations for a sumptuous volume, created for a princely library. As such
they acquired a place within the aristocratic court culture, albeit in a much
less conspicuous position than the great decorative cycles in Fontainebleau.
They do not ever enter the domain of the widely circulated printed image,
either, the so-called 'print culture' of the Early Modern period. The most
precise visual records of the image of the distant and unknown remained to a
large extent the property of elite classes and groups, and did not play a direct
role in the development of a generalized 'European vision' during the
Renaissance and baroque periods. Their relatively limited accessibility does
not reduce their importance for the history of art and culture. On the
contrary, the precious nature of the visual material enhanced its prestige and

value for the elite groups which formed the vanguard of artistic patronage in the sixteenth and seventeenth centuries.

As in the case of the Portuguese rutters, visual information in the *Rotz Atlas* and the works derived from it is presented in a synthetic fashion. In the sixteenth century the strict compartmentalization of knowledge and information did not exist. Nautical, geographical, ethnographical, botanical and zoological visual data could be compressed within the same space, resulting in dense pictographs conveying a complex image of a place. The elements of what Bernard Smith has called the typical landscape are already present. In contrast to the eighteenth-century formulation, they retain their own identity and do not merge into a harmonious totality.

While the maps and charts of the Dieppe school framed images of intense verisimilitude, they also contributed in no small way to the creation of the myth of Terra Australis in the sixteenth century. In contrast to the verismo of many of the vignettes pertaining to Africa, Asia, and America, the composite image of Java la Grande which can be drawn from the Dieppe maps and charts consists of a curious mélange of elements. A splendid example is the beautifully coloured world map of 1550 by Pierre Desceliers (figure 12).[11] A number of details are clearly meant to evoke the Sumatran environment. The thatched huts are vaguely similar to the habitations of Ticou depicted on the *Rotz* and *Vallard* atlases, but are far more generalized. They may be compared with very similar houses represented in Africa and Brazil on another masterpiece of Dieppe cartography, an atlas in The Hague dating from ca. 1545–47. The elephants may be Sumatran, while the group of men worshipping the sun may be Javanese. The long-necked, camel-like animals, on the other hand, are possibly guanacos from South America, first described by Pigafetta in his account of Magellan's voyage. These may have 'migrated' from Tierra del Fuego.[12] The dog-headed creatures are cynocephali, another of the monstrous races, that, according to Marco Polo, inhabited the islands of Andaman north of Nicobar. However, the acts of cannibalism performed by these beings in the vignette must have recalled the horrid contemporary accounts and images of South American Indians.[13] On the other hand, clusters of round dwellings may be compared with the homes of the Nguni-speaking people from the southeastern portion of Africa first encountered by the Portuguese in the fifteenth century.

The land of Java as pictured on the Dieppe maps constituted a fabulous, shadowy realm, filled with strange and exotic elements. These included a variety of animals, which may possibly represent wildlife from New Guinea and Australia. Swan-like creatures in the *Cosmographie Universelle* of Guillaume le Testu (1555) have been associated with Australian black swans; and flightless birds depicted in the same map, with the cassowary, found in the East Indies as well as Australia.[14] The latter would become coveted specimens for European *kunstkammern* (curiosity cabinets) of the seventeenth century, together with other animals to be later encountered in Australia, such as the wallaby and the fruit bat (flying fox).[15]

12 (and detail opposite) Pierre Desceliers, *Java la Grande*, 1550, MS., from his *World Chart*, by permission of the British Library (reproduced in colour following page 44)

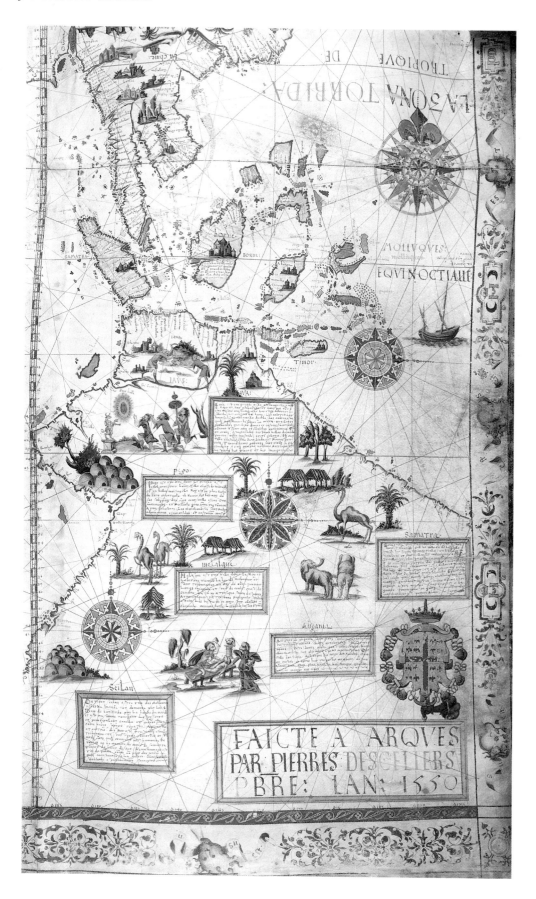

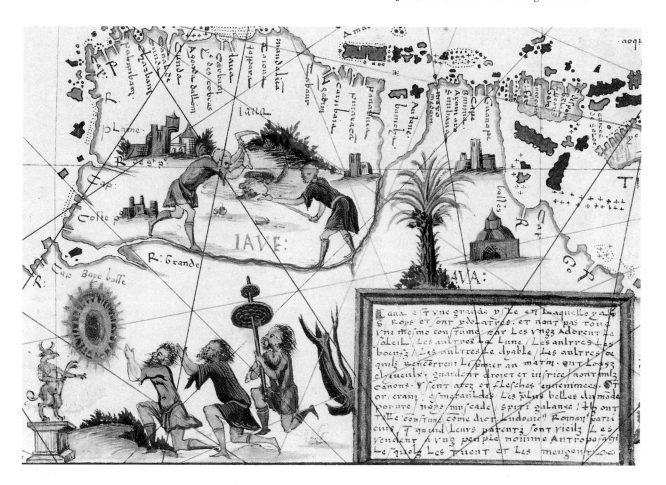

The images of birds on the Dieppe maps may be too fanciful to be positively identified. However, in Guillaume le Testu's world map of 1566, one of the last to depict Java la Grande, the artist has included the image of an animal which would symbolize the European fascination with Terra Australis: the bird of paradise. Le Testu's depiction is the first image of this creature to appear on a map.[16]

The Bird of Paradise

The island of New Guinea, the native habitat of certain species of the bird of paradise, had been discovered by the Portuguese navigator Jorge de Ménesès in 1526. The voyages of Alvaro de Saavedra in 1528 and Yñigo Ortiz de Retes in 1545 would provide charts of its northern coastline.[17] Its insularity would not be ascertained for many years, however; cartographers often assumed it to be a promontory of Terra Australis. The breeding grounds of the bird of paradise, in the interior of New Guinea, would in any case remain unexplored until the nineteenth century.

Specimens of the bird of paradise had reached Europe prior to the initial voyage to the shores of New Guinea.[18] Five were brought to Seville in the *Victoria*, the surviving vessel from Magellan's expedition, on 6 September 1522. These highly valued creatures, which were supposed to render their possessor invincible in battle, were acquired as gifts from the king of Batchian in the Moluccas. According to a letter written to the bishop of Salzburg by Maximilianus Transsylvanus, secretary of Charles V and an important source of information on Magellan's voyage, a specimen was presented to the emperor by the commander of the *Victoria*, Juan Sebastián del Cano. A faint but sensitively rendered silverpoint drawing by Hans Baldung Grien of a '*Paradisaea minor*' is said to depict one of the five birds brought to Spain by del Cano (figure 13).[19]

It was Maximilianus Transsylvanus who transmitted the legend of the bird of paradise to the West, a myth which would endure for centuries. In his letter to the bishop of Salzburg, published in Rome in 1523, the imperial secretary reported that the Moluccan rulers converted to Islam after hearing the legend. The creatures were thought to dwell amongst the immortal souls in the Earthly Paradise, remaining aloft during the course of their life and falling to earth only after death.[20] In the official account of Magellan's voyage, Antonio Pigafetta described the birds somewhat more objectively:

> These birds are as big as thrushes, with a small head and a long beak. Their legs are the length of a palm and thin as a pen. In place of wings they have long multicolored plumes resembling great panaches, whereas the feathers of the rest of the body are bronze-colored. Their tail is similar to that of a thrush and they fly only when there is wind. This explains why they would have come from the Earthly Paradise; because they call them 'bolon divita', which means 'birds of God'.[21]

13 Hans Baldung Grien, *Bird of Paradise*, ca. 1522 (?), silverpoint, Statens Museum for Kunst, Copenhagen

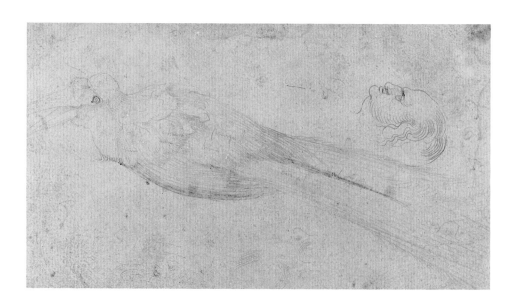

The specimens on the *Victoria* belonged to the species *Paradisaea minor* and were acquired on Tidore or Ternate. Presumably the wings were removed by hunters or traders, as we may surmise from Pigafetta's account. In the course of the following decade Portuguese navigators would obtain examples of the larger and more beautiful *Paradisaea apoda*. These were purchased in Ambon or Banda and came from the Aru Islands near New Guinea. The hunters from this region removed the animal's legs, as well as its wings, and it was in this mutilated condition that the birds arrived in Lisbon in the course of the fifth decade of the sixteenth century.[22] A number of specimens were obtained by prominent collectors, notably Conrad Peutinger of Augsburg and Melchior Guilandini of Padua. The great authorities in ornithology of the time, Conrad Gessner and Pierre Belon, were reliant upon drawings and accounts of these specimens to prepare their printed descriptions and illustrations.[23]

The absence of legs in these European specimens lent credence to the notion that the bird did not need and therefore did not have limbs, as it was constantly in flight. The theory was accepted and developed by the mathematician and physician Geronimo Cardano of Pavia. Copulation took place in flight, the male grasping the female with his long tail feathers. Furthermore, a cavity on the male's back enabled him to receive and incubate the egg. The birds were said to receive nourishment from the dew of heaven.[24] Cardano's ideas stemmed from antiquity, notably from Plutarch, who described a small bird from Persia known as a 'Rhyntakes', which lived on air and dew. Belon in his *L'histoire de la nature des oyseaux* identified the bird of paradise with this mythical creature.[25]

Other prominent scholars would further embellish the legend. Francesco López de Gomara believed that the bird lived on the sap of spice trees in addition to heavenly dew.[26] Conrad Gessner, who had not personally seen a specimen, accepted and elaborated upon the ideas of his contemporaries, adding that the bird could alight by wrapping its long tail feathers around a branch.[27] The animal entered the catalogue of the famous museum of Francesco Calzeoli in Verona as a 'Camaeleon aëreus' since, according to Pliny and Solinus, the chameleon received nourishment from the air.[28]

In the course of the sixteenth century the bird's features would be rendered in superb, brilliantly coloured images. These precise, accurate depictions of imperfect specimens did not resolve any scientific questions but merely contributed to the myth-making process. Perhaps the finest of these works is a sheet containing two watercolour drawings of the great bird of paradise, seen from above and from the side, in the Royal Museum of Fine Arts, Copenhagen (figure 14). The drawings are purportedly by the author of two animal studies in the same collection, one of which bears the monogram CA and the date 1567. The works in question were originally associated with Christoph Amberger, and subsequently with an obscure painter named Conrad Aicher, who was believed to have worked in Basel. The superbly finished watercolours are said to bear a close resemblance to the woodcut depiction of the bird in Gessner's *Vogelbuch*.[29] The relationship does not seem to be extremely close, however, and in any case the woodcut dates from 1555, or

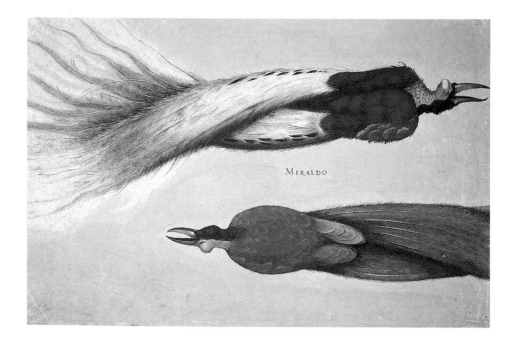

MIRALDO:

twelve years prior to the presumed date of the watercolours. The word
MIRALDO which appears on the sheet may well point towards an Italian
provenance, which is not unlikely as specimens of the bird could be seen in
prominent collections south of the Alps.[30]

In the early seventeenth century, one of the greatest naturalists of the
age, Carolus Clusius, wrote an account which specifically refuted the theory
of the legless bird of paradise. Clusius's discussion appeared in his renowned
work, the *Exoticorum libri decem* (1605), based upon evidence acquired
during the course of the first Dutch scientific voyage to the East Indies, the
expedition of Jacob van Heemskerck (1599–1601). Unfortunately, the high
monetary value placed upon the animal would prevent the naturalist from
obtaining a specimen to illustrate his work, and Heemskerck's bird was
purchased at a considerable price by Emperor Rudolf II.[31] In spite of
Clusius's efforts, the legend lived on for over two centuries; the animal
passed into the Linnaean nomenclature as the '*Paridisaea apoda*' or legless
bird of paradise. Not until 1824, when the French apothecary René Lesson
observed the bird in its habitat of New Guinea, was the myth finally
dispelled.[32]

The association of the animal with the Earthly Paradise, traditionally
believed to be situated somewhere to the east of the Asian landmass,
eventually led to its integration within the legend of Terra Australis. The
austral continent was regarded as a kind of paradise, an association
reinforced by accounts of Spanish discoveries in the South Pacific during the
second half of the sixteenth century. The incorporation – however tentative –
of New Guinea within the confines of the great southern continent led to the
selection of the bird as the symbol of a massive Terra Australis/Magellanica
at the end of the century.

The Map of Terra Australis

in the Sixteenth Century:

Mercator, Ortelius, Plancius

The explorations of Magellan, the contemporary discovery of the bird of
paradise, and the Parmentier voyages which gave rise to the legend of Java la
Grande, all contributed to a mosaic image of Terra Australis in the first half
of the sixteenth century. However, it was the great school of Netherlandish
cartographers that would establish a more or less standard configuration for
the southern continent. This image of a massive fifth continent would remain
in force until the mid-seventeenth century; afterwards it would be gradually
eroded by the findings of Dutch explorers.

The individual who fabricated the image of the southern continent for
generations of Europeans was Gerard Mercator (1512–94), the Flemish
geographer noted for the innovative two-dimensional projection of the earth's
surface which bears his name. In his terrestrial globe of 1541 dedicated to
Nicolas Granvelle, chief minister of Emperor Charles V, he designed a
massive austral continent, far more extensive than that which appeared on
an earlier version (1538) derived from the works of Schöner and Finé.

Twenty-eight years later, in 1569, Mercator explained his theories in
the tenth chapter of a treatise printed to accompany a new edition of his map
(figure 15) – essentially identical in form to his globe of 1541 – entitled *De
mundi creatione ac fabrica liber*. Reiterating the classical theorem, he argued
for an extensive southern landmass as a counterweight to the northern
hemisphere. Tierra del Fuego of Magellan is the pivotal zone, giving rise to
the name 'Magellanica', applied by Mercator to the entire continent.
Vespucci's land of parrots was completely detached from South America and
placed to the south of the Cape of Good Hope as 'Psittacorum regio'. New
Guinea is represented as an island, although Mercator notes that it is not
certain as to whether it is surrounded by water or constitutes a peninsula of
Terra Australis. In place of the Java la Grande of the Dieppe school he has
substituted the three rich East Asian kingdoms described by Marco Polo:
Beach, Lucach, and Maletur.[33]

Mercator's vision of the austral continent presented in his map of 1569
was replicated by Abraham Ortelius in his world atlas, *Theatrum Orbis
Terrarum*, published in Antwerp in the following year. Ortelius's work was the
first atlas of the world and was reprinted over a period of forty-two years. In
the title-page and the poem by Adolphus Mekerchus which accompanies it,
the promise of the unexplored Terra Australis is contrasted with the savage
and evil nature of the American continent.[34]

Christian Europe reigns supreme in the world-system represented and described by Ortelius and Mekerchus (figure 16). Enthroned above the architectural framework, she bears the imperial crown and sceptre, guiding the destiny of the world with a rudder surmounted by a cross. In clearly subsidiary roles Asia and Africa stand on plinths above the reclining naked

15 Gerard Mercator, *World Map*, 1569, Bibliothèque Nationale, Paris

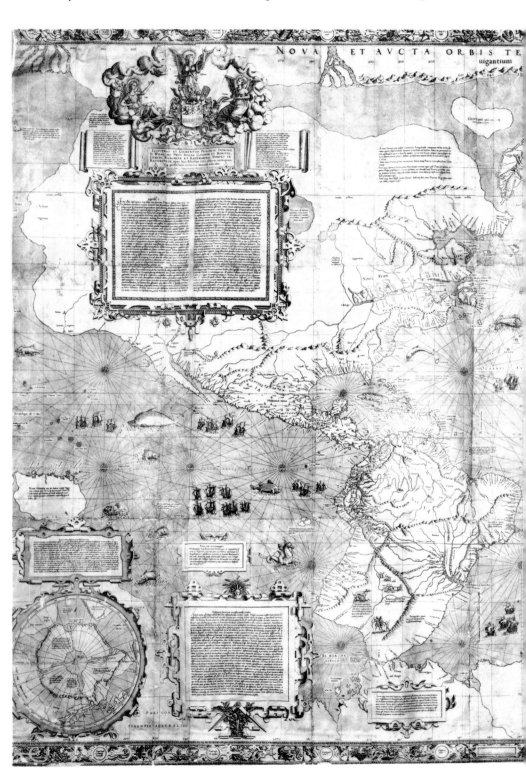

figure of America. The savage image of the fourth continent and the
accompanying text by Mekerchus were inspired by the popular account of
Brazilian cannibalism by the German traveller Hans Staden.[35] In her right
hand America holds the wooden club used to kill prisoners, in her left hand
a human head, symbolic of the flesh she has recently devoured.[36]

In close proximity to this horrific image is a herm, or bust, of a
beautiful maiden, representing Magellanica, the fifth continent, discovered
by Magellan on his voyage through the Strait. Beneath her breast is a flame
symbolizing the fires lit by the natives along the southern shore, observed
by Magellan's men: fires which inspired the name of the region, Tierra del

16 Title-page from
Abraham Ortelius,
Theatrum Orbis Terrarum,
by permission of the
British Library

Fuego.[37] In his explicatory Latin poem, Mekerchus extols the virtues of this mysterious virgin:

> Not far from here, the last nymph shows her bright head. Her face and
> looks are like a virgin's and she has a charming breast. Her hands and
> feet have been truncated, because she is hardly known to some people.
> The Iberian Magellan is said recently to have fallen in love with her,
> while he committed himself to the Austral wind in the Straits, and to
> have called her Magellanica after his own name. He happened to see
> the incautious virgin once, while flames were glittering from everywhere
> and while she was preparing solemn festivities. Therefore, the heavily
> blushing virgin immediately hid her face and concealed herself in a
> dark smoke in the shadows of a dull mist. But, in order not to be
> detected unawares again, she fixed this flame as a memory under her
> breast.[38]

In contrast to the unspeakably evil nature of America, the luminous image of the fifth continent represents a glimmer of hope. Mekerchus therefore ends his poem on an optimistic note, before inviting his readers to travel through the world via Ortelius's maps. Although the image of Terra Australis on the title-page of the *Theatrum Orbis Terrarum* is completely invented (in contrast to that of America, which includes certain authentic ethnographic data[39]), it coincides with the positive view of the fifth continent current at the time. If America was depraved and corrupted, perhaps the real Golden Land lay beyond its shores.

The image of Terra Australis created by Mercator was adopted with only minor variations by the 'father' of the great school of Dutch cartography, Petrus Plancius (1552–1622). Combining captured charts by the Portuguese cartographer Bartolomeo de Lasso with the Mercator map of 1569, Plancius created his own world maps as well as twenty-five navigational charts, published by Cornelis Claez in Amsterdam. The world map appeared in three editions: 1590, 1592, and 1594; the charts were printed in 1592.[40]

Plancius's planisphere of 1594 is elaboratedly decorated, with allegories of the parts of world depicted around its borders (figure 17). These include (on the upper border) Europe and Asia, and (below) Mexicana, Peruana, Magellanica, and Africa. The map presents an image of the world which was relatively unchanged from that which appeared on the maps of Mercator and Ortelius twenty-five years earlier. Among the few significant alterations is the addition of the Solomon Islands in the South Pacific, discovered by the Spanish explorer Alvaro de Mendaña y Neyra (1567–69, see chapter 5). These islands, whose exact configuration and location were not known for certain at the time, were believed to lie near the coast of the southern continent. New Guinea, represented as an island on the maps of 1590 and 1592, is depicted here as a promontory of Terra Australis; its insularity would in fact remain a matter of discussion until the time of Cook.

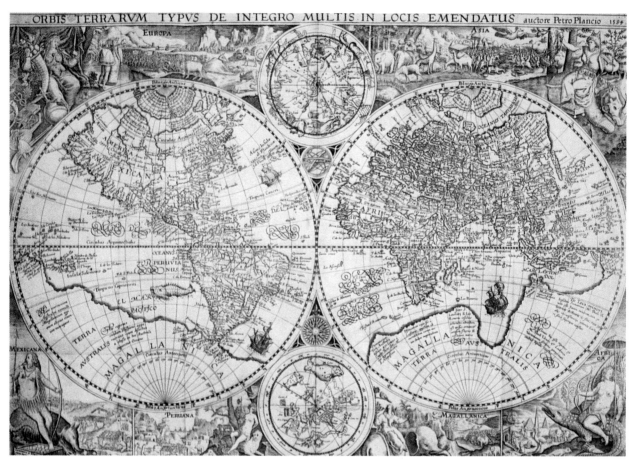

On his chart of the East Indies archipelago (figure 18), adapted from a map by de Lasso, Plancius represents New Guinea in more detail, asserting that it probably belongs to the southern continent: 'Partem autem esse continentis Australis magnitudo probabile facit'. On the lower border of the map, covering the landmass of Terra Australis are images of the products of the Indies: nutmeg, cloves, and sandalwood. The wealth of the Indies, therefore, is extended to New Guinea, which in turn merges with Terra Australis. These associations are embodied in the allegory of Magellanica on the lower border of the world map of 1594. A richly clad female figure, analogous to the image employed to symbolize Asia,[41] is depicted astride an elephant. In her right hand she holds a sprig of cloves and in her left hand, nutmeg. To the right, a bird of paradise hovers over a herd of elephants. The luminous but vague image of Magellanica in the *Theatrum Orbis Terrarum* has been transformed into something more splendid, linked with the material riches of Asia and the spiritual values embodied by the magical bird from the Earthly Paradise.[42]

Petrus Plancius's maps, together with the publications and explorations undertaken by Jan Huygen van Linschoten, would spearhead Dutch attempts to break the Portuguese monopoly over the spice trade. Plancius's world map of 1594 would appear in the various editions of Linschoten's account of his

18 Petrus Plancius,
*Chart of East Indies
Archipelago*, ca. 1593,
engraving, Algemeen
Rijksarchief, The Hague

voyage to the East, the *Itinerario, voyage ofte schipvaert …* (first edition
Amsterdam 1596; the Plancius map appeared in editions published from
1599 onwards). As Ernst van den Boogaart has noted, 'Plancius and van
Linschoten were leading figures in the preparations for the first Dutch
voyages to the East and West Indies. For them, the existence of a fifth
continent was more than just an interesting theoretical question; they made
it an objective of Dutch overseas expansion'.[43]

The Spanish Vision
of the Austral World:
Mendaña, Quirós, Torres

5

The allure of the southern continent glowed ever brighter in the course of the sixteenth century, principally as a result of the efforts of Spanish explorers in the South Pacific. Their voyages appeared to confirm the optimism of theoretical geographers in the Low Countries.[1]

By the mid-1560s Spain had already established itself as a Pacific power. The conquest of the Philippines in 1565 led to the establishment of an important trade route between New Spain and the western rim of the Pacific.

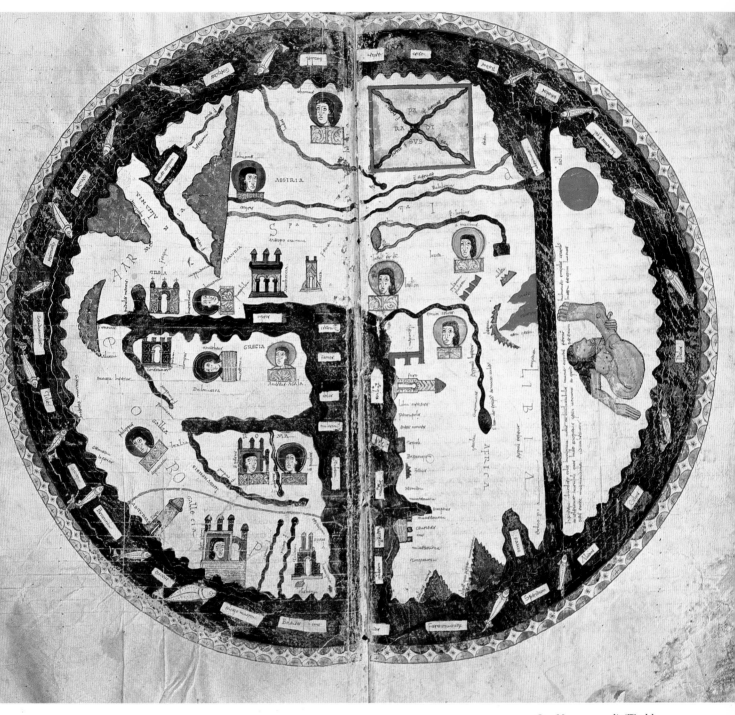

2 *Mappa mundi (World Map)*, 11th century, MS., *Osma Beatus*, Cathedral, Burgo de Osma

10 Jean Rotz, *Chart of Southeast Asia*, 1542, MS., from his *Boke of Idrography*, by permission of the British Library

Tzapobana

of ozient

Zeilon

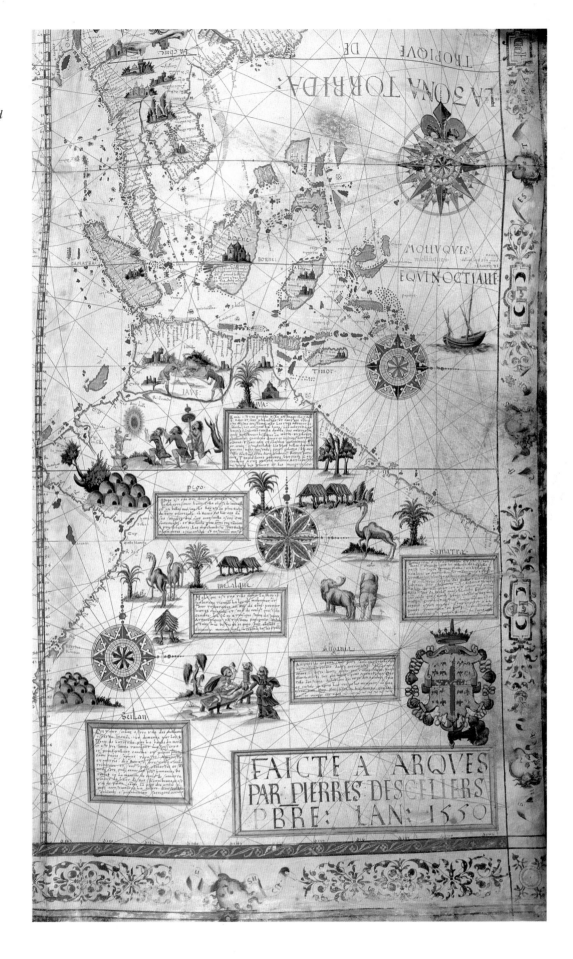

The Manila galleon set sail on a regular basis from Acapulco with its cargo of Mexican silver; it returned laden with goods from the East. New Spain's dominance of this lucrative route inspired the colonists of Peru to set sail from Callao towards the southwest in the hope of encountering other sources of wealth.

The government in Lima had reason to believe that great riches lay just beyond the horizon. In the first place they hoped to find the land of Ophir, source of the gold which the servants of Solomon had brought to Eziongeber, beside Eloth on the Red Sea. Its location constituted an age-old mystery: the Portuguese believed it would be found in East Africa, Columbus in Hispañola, Magellan in the Ryukyu Islands between Taiwan and Japan. Like the legendary kingdoms described by Marco Polo, it was generally thought to lie somewhere to the east – perhaps it might be found near the unknown southern continent.

Other rumours fuelled the Spanish imagination: in the Moluccas, an intriguing story circulated that the conqueror of Chile, Pedro de Valdivia, had information concerning an island kingdom, bordering a land of Amazons ruled by a queen called Guanomilla, or Golden Heaven. Unquestionably great riches would be found in this southern region. Then there was the story of Tupac Yupanqui's Inca fleet which sailed to islands rich in gold lying to the west of Peru, inhabited by black people. The desire for material gain stimulated by these tales, combined with a strong missionary zeal, would inspire three Spanish expeditions to the South Pacific and Terra Australis between 1567 and 1606.

In 1567 the governor of Peru, Garcia de Castro, appointed his nephew, Alvaro de Mendaña y Neyra, to command two ships which were to search for rich islands 'between New Guinea and this coast'. Cosmographer of the voyage was Pedro Sarmiento de Gamboa, author of *Historia de los Incas*, an important work on the indigenous people of Peru; the chief pilot was Hernán Gallego. It was Sarmiento's vision of rich western islands that provided the principal inspiration for the voyage; by contrast, Mendaña appears to have been mainly interested in the conversion of the natives. The expedition set sail from Callao on 19 November 1567; its apparent goal was to locate Sarmiento's islands, then the adjacent Terra Australis. On 7 February 1568 the explorers reached the Melanesian island of Santa Ysabel (Santa Isabel, in the Solomons), the largest Pacific island yet discovered by Europeans; at the Bahia de la Estrella they claimed 'las islas Salomón' for Philip II. Returning home shortly thereafter, the expedition reached Callao in September 1569.

The islands of King Solomon had apparently been found; the main objectives of the expedition, however, the acquisition of gold and the conversion of the natives, had not been achieved. Nor had the shores of Terra Australis been sighted and explored. Nevertheless, Sarmiento utilized his discoveries as evidence for the existence of a populated southern continent stretching from the east of Java to the Strait of Magellan. In the course of the expedition he prepared a vocabulary of Melanesian words, unfortunately lost, which supported his claims for ethnic ties between the inhabitants of the

Solomons and the peoples of South America, living across the strait from Magellanica.[2]

Upon reaching Peru, Mendaña sought support for a new voyage. In the interim, however, his uncle Garcia de Castro had been replaced as governor by Francisco de Toledo, who did not share his predecessor's enthusiasm for South Pacific exploration. Over a quarter of a century was to pass before a new expedition was outfitted to explore the Solomons and Terra Australis and to spread the Gospel in this remote part of the world. Mendaña was placed in command, this time with the Portuguese navigator, Pedro Fernández de Quirós, as chief pilot.

The explorers were frustrated in their efforts to build upon their previous successes. The Solomon Islands, discovered with such fanfare in 1568, could not be found in 1595. What the expedition did locate were the Marquesas, whose inhabitants were light-skinned Polynesians, not dark-skinned Melanesians. In the course of this encounter, the first significant contact between Europeans and Polynesians, two hundred natives were killed by the Spaniards. Mendaña was to meet his own end in the Melanesian island of Santa Cruz, situated to the southeast of the Solomon Islands; after many losses, the expedition reached the Philippines in 1597.

The tragic events of 1595–97 failed to weaken the resolve of the man who must be credited with the invention of the myth of a South Pacific/Australian paradise: Pedro Fernández de Quirós. The islands which he believed constituted part of Terra Australis, the New Hebrides (Vanuatu) – discovered in the course of his voyage of 1605–07 – would be integrated by geographers within the perimeter of the southern continent for over a century and a half. The accounts of his voyage and the numerous memorials written to gain support for explorations in South Pacific waters created an image of Terra Australis which would constitute a significant chapter in the history of Western utopias.

After a six-year effort to obtain funding (including an audience in Rome before Pope Clement VIII), Quirós finally received two ships and nearly 300 men from Philip III of Spain. Quirós commanded the *San Pedro*; the other ship was placed under the direction of another Portuguese navigator, Luis Váez de Torres, who was assisted by the aristocratic explorer Don Diego Prado de Tovar. The goal of the expedition was Terra Australis, thought to lie near the discoveries of 1568 and 1595. Quirós was convinced that such a continent necessarily existed in the vicinity of the well-populated Marquesas. Its relatively tranquil population, originating neither from New Spain nor the western shores of the Pacific, was believed to be ripe for colonization and conversion to Christianity.

Quirós and his companions set sail with great enthusiasm from Callao on 21 December 1605. The first inhabited islands visited by the expedition were in the Cook group. Quirós was greatly impressed by the beauty of the light-skinned Polynesians encountered there, calling the islands the 'Islas de Gente Hermosa'. His greatest discovery occurred on 1 May 1606. Quirós was convinced that he had reached the coasts of Terra Australis, the new

Promised Land, naming it La Austrialia del Espíritu Santo in honour of the
Spanish royal house of Austria; in reality he had landed in the New Hebrides
(Vanuatu). He travelled along its chief estuary, which he named the River
Jordan, certain that it constituted a river comparable to the Guadalquivir at
Seville. In the island's deep bay he founded the port of Vera Cruz and what
he hoped would be a great city, the New Jerusalem. Here he built a church of
boughs and plantains, established a municipality of thirty-four officers and
magistrates, and created a chivalric Order of the Holy Ghost in defence of
the natives. Quirós's ambitions and Christian zeal seemed to be boundless;
however, after an elaborate ceremony marking Corpus Christi, he abruptly
decided to set sail for home. The natives had not been as docile as
anticipated, and conflicts with the local inhabitants appeared to have
unnerved him. For whatever reason, the fleet left the islands on 8 June 1606.
In the course of a storm the two ships became separated from each other.
Quirós set off for Acapulco, reaching port after a journey of five months,
while Torres returned to the harbour of Vera Cruz. After waiting in vain for
fifteen days for Quirós to return, Torres initiated his momentous journey to
the northwest, through the strait separating Australia from New Guinea which
would eventually bear his name, prior to sailing to Manila via the Moluccas.

19 Diego Prado de
Tovar, *The Natives of the
Bay of San Felipe y
Santiago (Vanuatu),*
1606, watercolour,
Archivo General de
Simancas

The historical importance of Torres's journey was considerable, although for many years it constituted something of a postscript to the more well-known exploits of Quirós. The tip of Cape York, the northern extremity of the Australian continent, had most likely been sighted; yet, this discovery had no immediate repercussions. The voyage through the strait separating New Guinea from Australia was definite proof that New Guinea was an island; however, the existence of the passage was not universally accepted prior to Cook's first voyage.

The pictorial record of the Torres expedition likewise remained hidden for years. This consisted of a series of drawings by Prado de Tovar depicting the natives of Vanuatu, New Guinea, and the Torres Strait (figures 19–22).[3] Prado de Tovar was certainly not a draughtsman of great skill, yet he made a conscientious effort to differentiate the peoples he encountered. The dark-skinned natives of Vanuatu, leaves covering their genitals, are shown with their curved clubs, darts and arrows (figure 19). They are carefully distinguished from the comparatively light-skinned inhabitants of southeastern New Guinea, with their grass skirts, tattoos and round shields (figure 20). The Torres Strait Islanders are depicted in similar dress; a male warrior carries a club with a square end, perhaps the stone-headed *gaba-gaba* or *gaba-gaub* (figure 21). By contrast, the large quadrilateral shield borne by the inhabitants of southwestern New Guinea reveals the influence of Malay culture, transmitted by traders in the East Indies (figure 22).

Torres's prosaic account of his journey, and the drawings by Prado de Tovar which illustrate it are in stark contrast to the exuberant utopian image of Terra Australis evoked by Quirós in the account of his voyage and in more than fifty memorials addressed to the king of Spain in search of further support. Quirós never returned to the South Pacific and his dreams of an

20 Diego Prado de Tovar, *The Natives of the Bay of San Millán (Southeast New Guinea)*, 1606, watercolour, Archivo General de Simancas (reproduced in colour following page 76)

Iberian colony in the South Pacific died with him; nevertheless, his vision of the southern world would inspire generations of European writers and explorers.[4]

The arguments put forth by Quirós to support his hypothesis concerning Terra Australis were in part derived from traditional notions of terrestrial equilibrium: a southern landmass was required to balance those of the northern hemisphere. The age-old theory was bolstered by the evidence gathered by the explorer in the course of his journeys. In particular, the diversity of skin colour among the physically attractive inhabitants of the Solomons and Marquesas (white, black, mixed) indicated the presence of a continent, as did the vast rivers and high mountains discovered on Espíritu Santo. This landmass would be huge, equal in dimension to America as well as all of Europe and Asia to the Caspian Sea.

According to Quirós, conditions for European settlement of Terra Australis could not have been more favourable. The inhabitants were essentially peaceful in their relations with foreigners. Physically and morally superior to the American Indians, they would be more easily converted to Christianity if treated properly. A great port city could be established at Vera Cruz; the deep waters of its harbour could accommodate a thousand ships. The picturesque, varied landscape was supplied with abundant water, the beautiful vegetation of its forests emitted fragrant odours. The vigorous health of the natives and the presence of many elderly people resulted from the salubrious climate. Spanish settlers would not suffer from any illness, even if compelled to work very hard. There was in fact no significant obstacle to European settlement. The mountain slopes were free of snow; the lowlands contained none of the swamps, crocodiles, ants, caterpillars, mosquitos, or other hazards to human life found in the East Indies.

The fifth continent also surpassed the Indies in terms of its natural resources. Silver, gold, pearls, valuable oils, and coconuts were to be found in abundance. Its varied climate would permit the cultivation of European cereals in addition to spices. Salt and fish could be extracted from its seas. Native success with raising livestock could easily be imitated by Westerners. In short, if the Spice Islands had been denied to Spain, God had reserved for her an infinitely more desirable realm.

Quirós's utopian vision appears in its most concentrated form in his famous eighth memorial (first edition Madrid 1609). Within a decade it had been translated into all of the major European languages: Italian and German (1611), Dutch (1612), French and English (1617). The ideal of the Pacific paradise was invented by the Portuguese navigator, and the reverberations of Quirós's words may be felt in Bougainville's account of his visit to Tahiti in 1768, as described by Bernard Smith:

> 'One would think himself', wrote Bougainville, 'in the Elysian fields'. And he proceeded to write a description which stamped itself permanently upon the imagination of Europe. The country was so rich, the air so salubrious that people attained to old age without its inconveniences. Indeed, the island was a healer. Men rotten with scurvy regained strength after spending one night there. 'Everyone gathers fruits from the first tree he meets with, or takes some into any house he enters'.[5]

Bougainville's account is infused with an Ovidian pastoral lyricism characteristic of his time; the sentiments expressed in his words, however, seem to reflect the spirit of the eighth memorial of Torres. The ideal of Tahiti was not a creation of the Enlightenment, therefore, but a development upon a theme sounded a century and a half earlier.

Exotica in

Sixteenth-Century Spain

6

If, as I have indicated, the eighteenth-century myth of the Tahitian paradise must be examined in the light of the sixteenth-century Iberian legend of Terra Australis, the scientific voyages of the Enlightenment should also be viewed against the background of parallel expeditions undertaken in Renaissance Spain. Interest in depicting the peoples and natural phenomena of the non-European world was an important aspect of sixteenth-century visual culture: an interest that was strongly felt in Spain, as contemporary documents and texts clearly demonstrate.

The growing concern in the Iberian peninsula with producing accurate pictorial records of the world beyond Europe was reflected in the botanical studies of the Portuguese naturalist Cristóvão da Costa. In his illustrated volume, *Tratado de Las Drogas y Medicinas de las Indias Orientales*, first published in Spain (Burgos 1578), he criticizes his great predecessor Garcia de Orta, author of *Colóquios dos Simples, e Drogas e Cousas Medicinais da India* (Goa 1563) for relying entirely upon written descriptions of plants. Illustrations are valid in themselves, he argues; the texts, supplementary: 'The learned Dr Orta has written with curiosity and diligence, but he has used reports, whereas I have set down what I have seen with my own eyes and depicted from life'.[1]

Da Costa's words reflect an attitude which pervaded Spanish intellectual circles, nowhere more so than at the royal court. It was the king himself, Philip II, who instigated the first large-scale scientific expedition in which the visual arts played a major role: the voyage of the physician Francisco Hernández to Mexico (1571–76).[2] Hernández was instructed by the king to conduct a thorough investigation and to collect specimens and drawings of potentially useful plants. Borne in a litter carried by two mules, and accompanied by two or three artists, several writers, an interpreter and a number of plant collectors, Hernández travelled the length and breadth of New Spain in a series of five voyages. In spite of heat, cold, thirst, biting insects and untrustworthy informants, he was able to provide the king with fifteen volumes of illustrations and descriptions of thousands of plants and animals, together with seeds, medicines, dried plants, animal skins, and tubs containing live plants for acclimatization in the Old World. Regrettably, the illustrated volumes, which were housed in the Escorial library, were destroyed by fire in 1671.[3]

Hernández's interests were not limited to plants and animals. He marvelled at enormous bones and teeth unearthed at Toluca, fossils which he believed derived from an extinct race of giants. The pre-Conquest ruins of the royal palace at Texcoco deeply impressed him; he commanded his artists to reproduce the arms and military dress of two Aztec rulers, as well as the images of birds decorating one of the rooms. He also studied volcanic activity, describing the manner in which snow-capped peaks poured forth vast quantities of hot ash, lava, and pumice.[4]

Something of the wonder and amazement which Hernández's volumes must have inspired in his contemporaries is conveyed in a description of the manuscript by Fray José de Sigüenza, official historian of the Escorial. He states that the drawings depicted:

> all the animals and plants that one has been able to see in the West Indies, in their actual colors. The same color that the tree and the herb has, in its root, trunk, branches, leaves, flowers, fruits; also the color of the alligator, frog, snake, rabbit, dog, and the fish with its scales; the most beautiful feathers of so many different varieties of birds, their feet and beaks and also the forms, colors and dress of the men, and the

ornaments of their dress and their festivals and the manner of their
meetings and dances and sacrifices – altogether, something which
furnished delight and variety in the viewing.[5]

Hernández's volumes were illustrated by three Mexican artists: Antón and
Baltasar Elías and Pedro Vázquez. The king was so impressed by these
images of the New World that he wished to surround himself with them. The
result was a decorative cycle which may have been unique in European art of
the time. Twenty-three paintings based upon the works of Hernández's artists
decorated the chamber and gallery of the king in the Escorial.[6] A number of
sources attest to the presence of these paintings, including Sigüenza, who
notes (in regard to the gallery):

> It also contains many different paintings which are worth considering:
> portraits from nature of many things that one sees in our Indies, some of
> the many different birds with the actual colors of their feathers, others
> of a variety of large and small animals ...[7]

The artist responsible for the works in the king's chamber was Fray Juan de
San Jerónimo. According to his epitaph:

> He knew how to illuminate and understood practical perspective, and
> executed the canvases of herbs and animals which are in the room of
> His Majesty. Those depicting the herbs are extremely elaborate images:
> from leaf to tree, from tree to root, they appear to be nothing but actual
> likenesses. They would be of great value if they were bound in a
> volume, because the originals were the herbs of the Indies from which
> Doctor Francisco Hernández composed the precious books which are in
> the library. Our Fray Juan assumed this task to please His Majesty, who
> loved to see the pictures of the birds and animals of the Indies which
> are in these works, and also because he was afraid that these loose
> sheets may be easily lost.[8]

One would wish to know more regarding the drawings in Hernández's volumes
and the paintings which were based upon them, all of which were lost in the
Escorial conflagration of 1671. The episode in any case indicates that the
efforts of Cook and his artists and scientists relate to an older tradition.
Knowledge of Hernández's arduous but productive overland journeys leads
us to question the assertion that the 'floating laboratories' of the eighteenth
century brought about a new image of nature and man, whereas the interiors
of continents remained unknown.[9] Also, the hypothesis that the scientific
illustrations created on Cook's voyages brought about a new emphasis on
naturalism in the visual arts must be questioned. Fascinated with the art
of Dürer, his contemporaries and successors in northern Europe, Philip II
and his court were understandably delighted with the work of Hernández,
his artists and their copyists. We should not be surprised to learn that the

king commissioned replicas of these pictures. These decorations would have had an obvious political function, glorifying the greatness and extent of the king's domains. Whether these representations had any impact on later manifestations of the same phenomena, for example the works commissioned by Johan Maurits in Brazil during the 1630s and 1640s (see chapter 9), is not known; however, the possibility should not be ruled out.

Art, Science and Exploration in Elizabethan England

7

The interest in depicting the plants, animals, and native inhabitants of the world beyond Europe manifested itself not only in Iberia but in England, the great rival of the Spanish empire. In the case of the latter, we are fortunate in possessing a significant fragment of the visual record, in the form of images by and after the artist-explorer John White, executed in the lost colony of Roanoke (present-day North Carolina). These monumental works of observation constituted an extraordinary moment in the history of Renaissance art and a remarkable precedent for the artists employed on English voyages two centuries later.

John White's memorable drawings constitute a logical development in the history of art and exploration in the British isles. Unquestionably, the greatest English navigator of the age, Sir Francis Drake, was acutely aware of the importance of accurate draughtsmanship. The 'famous voyage' (1577–80) of Drake, the freebooter and, later, one of the leaders of the fleet which defeated the Spanish Armada, was the first English circumnavigation of the globe. Sailing around the tip of South America, Drake passed directly up the west coast of the Americas to California, then across the Pacific to the Moluccas. The objectives of the expedition are not known for certain, although some scholars have thought that one of its goals was to explore Terra Australis. In any event, the voyage had significant repercussions for the history of the legendary fifth continent. Sailing to the southern tip of America, Drake discovered that there was no continental mass connected to Tierra del Fuego, only a group of islands. On a map drawn after an original by Francis Fletcher, one of Drake's companions, illustrating a copy of Fletcher's journal, these islands are labelled with the ironic epithet 'Terra australis bene cognita'. However, the existence of this passage around the tip of South America remained controversial for forty years after Drake's voyage; it was confirmed only after the expedition of Jacob le Maire and Willem Schouten to the South Pacific (1615–17).[1]

Like Jean Rotz (whose atlas in the Royal Library he conceivably might have known), Drake was convinced of the utility of drawing in navigation and exploration. According to the testimony of Nuno da Silva, a Portuguese captive of the famous navigator:

> Francis Drake kept a book in which he entered his navigation and in which he delineated birds, trees and sea-lions. He is an adept at painting and has with him a boy, a relation of his [his cousin, John Drake], who is a great painter. When they both shut themselves up in his cabin they were always painting.[2]

Another of Drake's prisoners, Don Francisco de Zárate, wrote:

> He also carries painters who paint for him pictures of the coast in its exact colours. This I was most grieved to see, for each thing is so naturally depicted that no one who guides himself according to these paintings can possibly go astray.[3]

No drawings by Drake or by artists on his voyage around the world are known to survive. However, Francisco de Zárate's memoir is corroborated by an extant illustrated rutter of Drake's final expedition to the West Indies in 1595–96, recording precise details of coastlines in the Caribbean.[4]

Some indication of the subject matter rendered by Drake and his artists can be discerned through an examination of the illustrations in the Fletcher

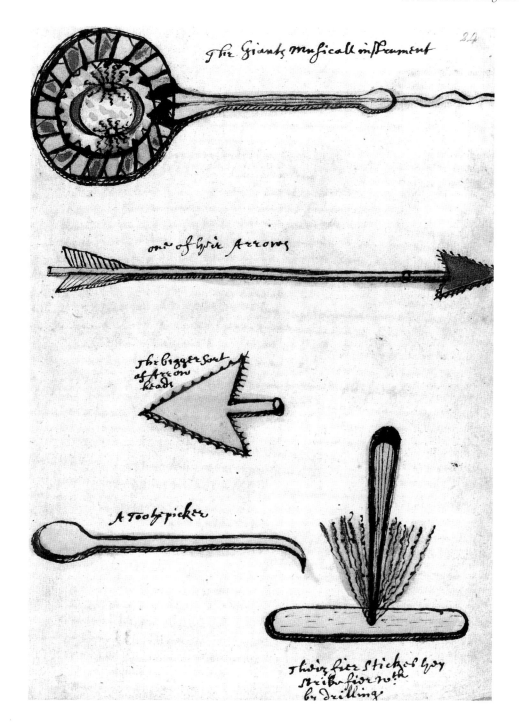

The Giants Musicall instrument

one of their Arrows

The bigger sort of Arrow heads

A Toothpicker

Their fier stickes they strike fier with by drilling

23 After Francis Fletcher, *Indian Artefacts from the Tierra del Fuego*, 1677 (after originals from 1577), MS., by permission of the British Library

manuscript. The drawings are derived from Fletcher's copies of the original sketches by Drake and his cousin John (figure 23).[5] These represent animals, birds, and Indian artefacts, including musical instruments, implements and weapons. Crude as they are, they provide some valuable information regarding the material culture of the inhabitants of Tierra del Fuego and Patagonia: the Telhuce and Yahgan Indians. They also attest to the thoroughness of Drake's investigations.[6] At the same time the drawings and text give us useful insights into the nature of the ethnography of the time, and its relationship with the global power struggle between Spain and its Protestant adversaries.

The belief that the inhabitants of the region were giants originated in Pigafetta's account of Magellan's voyage, and Fletcher lent credence to the persistent tale of a monstrous race inhabiting the antipodes. Yet the Patagonians, regardless of their stature, were by no means inhuman in their behaviour:

> ... showing themselves not only harmless, but also most ready to do vs anny good and Pleasure yea they shewed vs more kindenes than many christians would have donn ...[7]

Patagonian attacks on Drake and his men, in Fletcher's view, were not caused by an inherent brutality but rather by a long-standing grudge against Europeans, provoked by perfidious Iberian Catholics decades earlier:

> ... for when Magilanus was there he injuriously tooke from these people 2 of their men and that with violence, to the shedding of blood and murther on both sides, which wrought in them such a dislyke that they purposed and vowed revenge if ever tyme and opertunity serued.[8]

Fletcher's explanation of Indian behaviour is compatible with the fiercely anti-Spanish tone of his journal. We should, therefore, evaluate his generally favourable statements concerning Indian material culture as a means of bolstering his arguments against alleged Spanish barbarism. His drawings, the earliest visual records of the inhabitants and their cultural artefacts, give further credence to his views.

The English traveller reserved his strongest praise for the canoes of the Tierra del Fuegans:

> Touching their Boates they being made of large Barke instead of other Timber. They are most artificiall & of the most fine proportion with a starne & foreship standeing vp semicirculer wise & welbecometh the vessel ... we found not the like Boates at anny tyme for forme & fine proportion, in the sight & vse whereof princes might seeme to be delighted the forme whereof I have sett forth as neere as I could take it.[9]

Native craft from the southernmost regions of the world constituted evidence of an intelligent people who might prosper if freed from Spanish tyranny and placed under Protestant guidance. Direct comparisons of native and European technology, which might support such arguments, would be facilitated by museums within a few decades. In the cabinet of the English Royal Society, for example, an Eskimo kayak was exhibited together with a double-hulled craft designed by Sir William Petty.[10]

John White

Although little remains of the visual record of Drake's explorations, it is clear that pictorial representation constituted an important aspect of his voyages. By the early 1580s, in fact, draughtsmen were beginning to fulfil an important role on English voyages. This was already the case in Spain, as we have seen. In France, as well, an important precedent had been set in the course of the expedition of the Huguenot René de Laudonnière to Florida (1563–65). Jacques le Moyne de Morgues, a noteworthy botanical draughtsman, accompanied the voyage and prepared a comprehensive set of illustrations of the daily life and military activities of the Timucua Indians, in addition to an important series of maps. Although nearly all of the original drawings are lost, engravings after his studies by Theodor de Bry published in 1591 give us an indication of their variety and quality. Le Moyne moved to England in the 1580s, where his work and his example would have a significant impact upon the artistic activities of John White in America.[11]

The value placed upon illustration within the circles of Sir Walter Raleigh, the driving force behind the Roanoke expedition, is revealed in the instructions given to Thomas Bavin, the artist who accompanied the voyage of Raleigh's half-brother, Sir Humphrey Gilbert, to Newfoundland in 1582. In addition to preparing a series of detailed maps, Bavin was to:

> … drawe to lief one of each kinde of thing that is strange to us in England … all strange birdes beastes fishes plantes hearbes Trees and fruictes … also the figures & shapes of men and women in their apparell as also the manner of weapons in every place as you shall find them differing.[12]

Gilbert's instructions to his artist (whose work has not survived) may well have been identical to the lost directives given to John White prior to his departure for America in 1585. In any event the nature of the works executed by the artist corresponds exactly to what was required of Bavin. With an extraordinary degree of precision White rendered the images of the men, women, and children of Roanoke, their homes, villages, funerary practices, cuisine, eating habits, agriculture, fishing, and so on. In his images of the Indians themselves the artist has endeavoured to render their facial features, body decoration, and colouring as faithfully as possible. The result was a series of extremely valuable drawings. William Sturtevant has observed that, 'There is no comparable set of illustrations by a single hand dealing with one small culture area anywhere in North America before the age of photography'.[13]

White's natural history studies are likewise of extremely high quality, notably his images of hermit crabs, fireflies, fish, and turtles. In his versatility he compares favourably with the artists accompanying Cook. In a remarkable study of Indians fishing, images of aquatic life are incorporated into a lively, atmospheric river landscape conveying the character of American waters prior to English settlement (figure 24). White's drawing may well be viewed in certain respects as a precedent for the 'typical' landscape. However, in conformity with the mentality of the period, the elements in his composition retain their integrity as separate entities, like the specimens in a curiosity cabinet or the decorations of a Renaissance map.

24 John White, *Indians Fishing*, 1585, watercolour, Department of Prints and Drawings, copyright British Museum

The most extraordinary aspect of White's work is the conscientious manner in which the artist attempted to render cultural differences pictorially. In this sense he fulfilled the objectives outlined in Bavin's instructions. It was precisely this subtlety which is lost in the engravings made after his work by Theodor de Bry. These prints appeared as illustrations to a text by Thomas Harriot, the scientist who accompanied White, published by de Bry as *A briefe and true report of the new found land of Virginia* (Frankfort 1590). Paul Hulton has praised the high quality of the de Bry engravings and their faithfulness to the originals;[14] I would agree with the first point but not the second. White's depiction of an Indian man and woman eating, for example, has been beautifully rendered but significantly altered by de Bry. In White's drawing (figure 25)[15] the man squats in the characteristic Indian manner; in de Bry's engraving (figure 26)[16] his legs are extended in what would have been considered as a more graceful, European fashion. His companion's face has been considerably idealized, as she turns to regard the spectator in a coy manner. White's effort to represent a different culture depended largely upon these subtle details, which have been carefully and deliberately excised by de Bry's engravers. This alteration resulted in an image which may have been thought to be more suitable to the text. In Harriot's caption to the engraving as published by de Bry, the scientist

25 John White, *Indian Man and Woman Eating*, 1585, watercolour, Department of Prints and Drawings, copyright British Museum

26 After John White, *Indian Man and Woman Eating*, 1590, engraving from T. Harriot, *A briefe and true report of the new found land of Virginia*, by permission of the British Library

emphasizes the restrained and dignified eating practices of the Indian couple: 'They are verye sober in their eatinge, and trinkinge, and consequentlye very long lived because they doe not oppress nature'.

The most radical alterations were perpetrated upon one of the most complex of all of White's images: 'Indians dancing' (see figures 27–28). The artist's many pentimenti are indicative of the problems he must have faced. As Hulton has observed:

> To convey the sense of movement in his drawing of the dance-scene was surely a most difficult challenge to his ability. Yet he succeeds in suggesting that their sudden jerky motions have been frozen only for an instant and that they are about to resume them. The movements were no doubt entirely strange to him and probably differed more from his own experience of English dancing than the modern dance would differ to us from classical ballet.[17]

It is perhaps presumptuous to speculate as to the range of White's knowledge of the dance in England; possibly the Morris dancers of the time provided him with a spectacle that was just as vigorously performed, if obviously of a different order.[18] In any case much of White's concerted effort to extract the

27 John White, *Indians Dancing*, 1585, watercolour, Department of Prints and Drawings, copyright British Museum

essence of the Indian performance has been lost in the translation to the print medium. The movement of the dancers is more regular and subdued; the three women who warmly embrace each other in the centre of the circle have been replaced by the Three Graces.

In his series of publications known as the *Great Voyages*, the most extensive set of illustrated volumes on the Americas, the strongly anti-Catholic de Bry presented a damning picture of Spanish enterprises in the New World.[19] The hellish image of Spanish America, replete with murderous conquistadors and savage cannibals presented in the majority of these volumes contrasts with the more restrained portrayal of the Indians visited by White and his companion and colleague, Thomas Harriot. Harriot's text, published by de Bry as the first volume of his *Great Voyages* celebrates English efforts at colonization in North America. It was entirely appropriate, therefore, for the Indians of Roanoke to be represented and described as a people on a higher level, ripe for conversion by benevolent Protestant settlers. The extremely subtle nuances contained in White's originals were not reproduced. Accessible to only a select few, they reflect a distinct sensibility and mentality.

28 After John White,
Indians Dancing, 1590,
engraving from T. Harriot,
*A briefe and true report of
the new found land of
Virginia*, by permission of
the British Library

Much more has been said, and will be said, regarding White's
drawings. I have discussed them at some length as evidence of the extremely
sophisticated cultural level of visual culture which facilitated the enterprise
of exploration and discovery in England two centuries before Cook. The
products of this culture could, however, be fully appreciated only by the
comparatively limited numbers of people with access to original works. This
discontinuous process of selective, limited dissemination of illustrative
material characterizes the entire history of art and exploration in the Early
Modern world.

Part

The Southern World in the Age of Dutch Expansion: 1606–1756

II

The Dutch Image

of the Southland

8

Prado de Tovar's drawings on the Torres expedition constitute the earliest visual images of the inhabitants of what was thought to be Terra Australis. By contrast, no artist was present on the voyage of the Dutch vessel *Duyfken* to Cape York in 1606. No journal or contemporary map survives from this historic voyage, the earliest documented European expedition to Australia. Yet, during the seventeenth century and early eighteenth century the Netherlands shaped the image of the South Pacific, Australia, New Guinea, and New Zealand, its lands and people – prior to the first voyage of Cook in 1768. Sailing under the auspices of the Dutch East India Company, the world's most powerful economic organization for over a century following its founding in 1602, a significant number of Dutch vessels played a role in the search for Terra Australis (or, as it was often called, the Southland). Some were part of expeditions launched specifically to explore the fifth continent; still others reached the western shores of Australia by accident, blown off course on their way to Java.

The Southland was situated at the fringes of the Dutch eastern mercantile empire, a network of trading posts and colonies stretching from the Cape of Good Hope to the Moluccas. In the course of the first half of the seventeenth century, the Dutch supplanted the Portuguese as the dominant European power in the region. For a period of 150 years they sought, intermittently, to incorporate the Southland into this zone. Their efforts came to nothing; the region was too remote, its riches too difficult to exploit. The resources of the small country were strained to the limit. The decline of Dutch power at the end of the eighteenth century paved the way for the great European mercantile nations, England and France, to assume the major role in exploring and colonizing the area.

For over a century, however, Dutch navigators mapped the coastlines of Australia, New Guinea, and a number of South Pacific islands. As a result of their efforts the outline of the Australian landmass, with the exception of the east coast discovered by Cook, became visible. In addition, Dutch draughtsmen produced the first images of the coastal land-features of Australasia, as well as depictions of the people of the region (Horne Islanders, Tongans, Maoris, Papuans) and aspects of its natural history. Plants, animals, and ethnographic specimens from the area found their way into collections in the Netherlands and elsewhere in Europe. A number of images based upon this research appeared in the form of engravings, serving as 'visual aids' for Banks and his colleagues on Cook's first voyage. The reproductions consulted by Banks were however, considerably altered in respect to their original, seventeenth-century appearance. The experience of Dutch explorers in the Southland was only partially transmitted to their successors.

The graphic records of Dutch voyages in search of Terra Australis in the first half of the seventeenth century are evidence of the important function of drawing in expeditions undertaken by the Netherlands. From the outset the Dutch East India Company required detailed written reports from its agents overseas; these were to be supplemented by graphic material. The precise nature of the observations to be made was outlined in the instructions to merchants and officials in the Company service. Agents were expected to describe, or draw on a map, specific aspects of the geography and topography of the rivers, towns, and ports, as well as important plants and fruits. In addition, they were to provide reports and/or drawings pertaining to a locality's government, criminal justice system, weaponry, religious ceremonies, clothing, marriage customs – in short, anything that might aid the Company in the conduct of its affairs. All drawings, sketches, maps, and reports were to be turned over to the Company directors.[1] We should remember also that what we may describe as ethnographic material, especially weaponry, was likewise collected as documentary evidence.

Dutch Australian

Expeditions: 1606–36

9

The European discovery of Australia, by Willem Jansz in 1606, was an event of global significance. Yet, whereas every schoolchild knows that Columbus arrived in America in 1492, in Australia neither the date of the country's discovery nor the name of the discoverer are universally known. The reasons for this apparent anomaly are not difficult to ascertain. In the first place, Jansz's Dutch nationality precluded any lasting fame in Anglo-Saxon Australia. Equally important, perhaps, his expedition lacked the heroic scale of the voyage of Cook, or even of Torres or Tasman. The voyage which may

MIRALDO:

14 Master CA (with the acorn), *Two Birds of Paradise*, ca. 1567, watercolour, Statens Museum for Kunst, Copenhagen

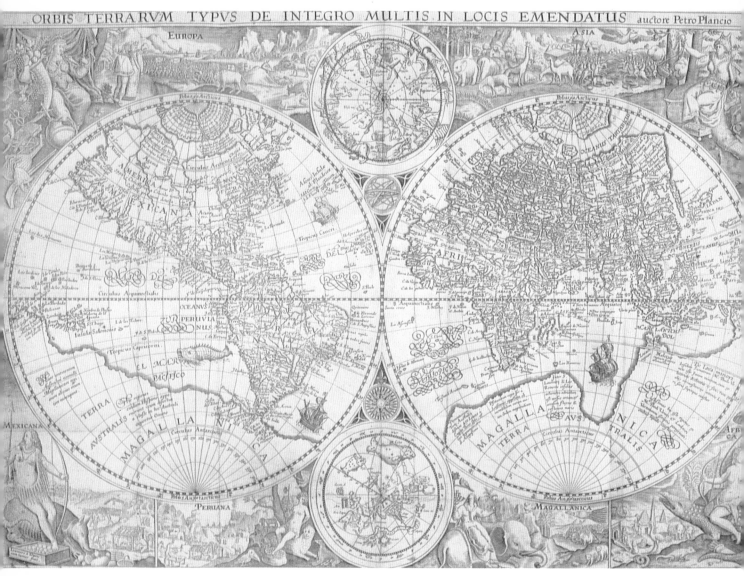

17 Petrus Plancius,
World Map, 1594,
engraving, by permission
of the British Library

be said to have ended the centuries-old search for Terra Australis was a comparatively short, relatively undramatic journey from Bantam in the East Indies to the Cape York Peninsula. The unspectacular nature of the event may have constituted a motivation for scholars to attempt to find a Portuguese antecedent for Jansz.

The discovery of Terra Australis resulted from the initiative of a minor Dutch official, Jan Willem Verschoor, director of the Bantam factory of the Dutch East India Company or, properly, the Verenigde Oostindische Compagnie (VOC). Wishing to test the veracity of rumours of trade opportunities and gold in the uncharted waters lying to the southeast of the Spice Islands, in November 1605 he sent the yacht *Duyfken* commanded by Jansz, to the south coast of New Guinea. After the loss of eight men in a violent encounter with the natives, the vessel crossed what was thought to be a gulf (actually the Torres Strait) and landed at the mouth of the Pennefather River, Cape York, in March 1606. Shoals prevented the Dutch vessel from entering the passage, which would be explored by Torres several months later. The expedition continued southwards for 200 miles along what they believed to be a portion of the New Guinea coast, losing another member of the crew in a skirmish with the Aborigines at the Batavia River before turning back.[1] The event was recorded by an Englishman, John Saris, resident in Bantam, who noted that 'in sending their men on shoare to entreate of Trade, there were nine of them killed by the Heathens, which are man-eaters; so they were constrained to returne, finding no good to be done there'.[2] In this terse and gloomy phrase, the 'Southlanders', Papuans and Aborigines alike, entered into the European consciousness. The earliest-known graphic image of Australia produced as a result of this voyage, appears in a finely coloured chart of the *Duyfken*'s route, bound within the folio leaves of the magnificent *Atlas van der Hem* in Vienna (figure 29).[3] In the monumental wall map of the Pacific Ocean by Hessel Gerritsz (1622) the tip of a great continent, designated as 'Nueva Guinea', appears lost within the enormous expanse of sea.[4]

The VOC, absorbed in the struggle for dominance in the East Indies with its Portuguese, Spanish, and English rivals, did not launch any further expeditions to the Southland for the next seventeen years. The only sightings of the Australian coast during this period were accidental: the result of ships sailing too far to the east prior to turning north towards Batavia, capital of the Dutch Indies, following the route devised by Hendrik Brouwer in 1611. The most noteworthy of these accidental sightings was the arrival on the west coast of Dirck Hartogsz on the *Eendracht*, marked on Hessel Gerritsz's map of the Indian Ocean (1622) as 'landt van d'Eendracht' and 'Dirck Hartogs ree (roadstead)'. In 1619 Frederik de Houtman and Jacob Dedel, on the *Dordrecht* and *Amsterdam*, reached the continent's western shores; Houtman's Abrolhos remains the name of the island discovered on this voyage.[5]

The most extraordinary 'Australian' expedition of the period never reached the actual continent, nor was it organized by the VOC. It was launched, instead, by a bitter rival: the Australian Company of Isaac le Maire

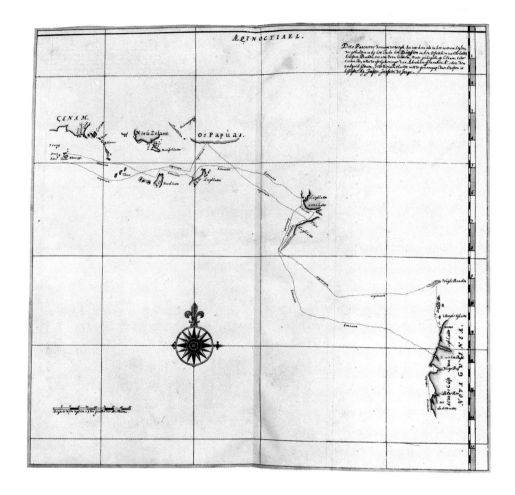

(1558/9–1624).⁶ One of the early directors of the VOC, le Maire resigned
after having been accused of fraud. In 1614 he founded his own organization
to find a passage south of Tierra del Fuego to the Pacific and to explore
Terra Australis. By sailing from east to west, he hoped to challenge the
VOC's monopoly on eastern and Pacific trade (the eastern routes round the
Cape of Good Hope were reserved for the East India Company). Le Maire's
flotilla set sail in 1615, led by his son Jacob, assisted by Willem Cornelisz
Schouten. Prior to reaching the southern tip of the Americas, the eighth
memorial of Quirós was read to the officers. The utopian vision of the
Catholic navigator was a beacon of inspiration for his Protestant successors –
a vision which would be enriched by the words and images produced by the
le Maire expedition.

Sailing through the passage located south of Tierra del Fuego, le Maire
confirmed the results of Drake's expeditions. As a result, the imagined
mainland of Terra Australis in the western hemisphere was moved further
south; an island thought to be a promontory of the continent was designated
as the Statenland. Once in the Pacific, the expedition travelled northwest into
Polynesia. On 9 May le Maire and Schouten became the first Europeans to
reach the Tongan islands, specifically the northern detached islands of Tafahi
and Niuafou. Miscalculating their longitude, the Dutch believed that they had

arrived in the vicinity of Quirós's 'southern continent'; in reality they were much further to the east.[7] Here, the explorers paused to admire and record the form of a native canoe, presumably bound for Samoa; this image of a Polynesian vessel, the earliest to be rendered in detail, would have a long afterlife in the imagery of the Pacific.[8] Ten days later the Dutch reached the Horne Islands, Futuna and Alofi; in the course of this visit the initial Dutch impressions of the South Pacific were formed.

The verbal–visual image of Polynesia which emerges from le Maire's account is generally favourable, although misgivings regarding native morality are clearly expressed. The Dutch encounter with the people of Futuna is depicted in a crudely drawn but detailed engraving, most likely derived from first-hand sketches (figure 30).[9] In the background, two 'chiefs' or 'kings' prostrate themselves before each other, in front of a conical native dwelling. In the middle distance the next episode in the narrative is shown. The two 'rulers' are represented side-by-side in the *belay*, or 'royal pavillion', in a remarkable juxtaposition of baroque spectacle and exoticism. The text describes the scene as follows:

> As they [the kings] were about to sit down they recited their prayers
> again, according to their wont, with their heads hanging down, bowing

30 *Horne Islands (Futuna)*, 1618, engraving from Jacob le Maire, *Oost ende West-Indische Spieghel*, Mitchell Library, State Library of New South Wales

to the ground and clapping their hands together, all of which was wonderful for us to behold. Our clerk, Aris Claesz, having already proceeded ashore in the forenoon, Jacob le Maire and Claesz Jansz Ban were also invited in the afternoon. They went ashore, taking with them four trumpeters and a drummer, and came to the kings; they blew on the trumpets together and beat the drums before both kings, who were seated together and took exceeding pleasure therein.[10]

If the Dutch enjoyed this rather strange form of musical entertainment, they took a much less positive view of the succeeding phase of the spectacle, depicted in front of the *belay*:

After that [the concert] a number of peasants from the smallest island came to the kings, bringing with them a quantity of green herbs, which they called kava … and commenced all together to chew those herbs with their mouth. When these had been chewed quite small they took them out of their mouth and placed all this together in a big wooden trough, poured water upon it, stirred and kneaded it together, and gave it to the kings, who drank thereof with the nobles. They also offered it to our men, but these had more than enough at the sight of it.[11]

The sharp contrast between the attractive and repulsive aspects of Futuna is further exemplified in the foreground figural group, wherein the beauty of the men is juxtaposed with the hideousness of the women. The 'ruler' is represented together with his 'nobles', an unusual figure to be sure, with a long braid hanging down below his waist – yet dignified as well, hand on hip, gesticulating with a commanding gesture. The image corresponds to the positive textual image of the island's male inhabitants:

The people of that island [Futuna] were stout-hearted folk and tall of stature, for the ordinary men amongst them were no shorter than the tallest of ours, whilst the tallest of them stood out far above the latter. They were strong men and very well made in body and limb; they could run very swiftly and swim and dive in masterly fashion. They were quite a brownish yellow in colour, were intelligent, and adorned their hair in very different ways; some had it curled, others beautifully crimped …[12]

The contrast between the descriptions of the men and the women (represented by the seated mother and child to the left of the 'king'), could not have been greater:

The women were very unsightly, both in face and body, with their hair cut short, like the men in Holland; they had long hanging breasts, which, in some, hung down like empty bags as far as their belly. They were very unchaste and allowed themselves to be used in all men's presence, even close to the king, with only a small mat over them.[13]

Certainly, we are very far from the enticing image of the Polynesian woman so
familiar to us from eighteenth-century travel books. The representation of
physical degeneracy among the women of Futuna is directly transposed from
the textual comments on their supposed immoral sexual behaviour. The
resultant image is related to the contemporary European stereotype of the
witch, whose unchaste sexual mores were associated with the visual motif of
grotesque, sagging breasts.[14] In a different context, one which is not explicitly
sexual, we find no references to physical deformity: for example, the account
of female dancers performing before the 'king' – a description comparable to
those written by eighteenth-century explorers in the South Pacific:

> In the evening we went to the king; there we found a number of
> maidens dancing naked before the king. One of them played upon a
> piece of hollow wood like a pump that gave forth sound, whereupon
> these maidens danced very prettily and entertainingly and with much
> grace to the measure of that music, so that our people were surprised to
> see the like among savage folk.[15]

The context modifies the perception and imagery; in the festive ceremony
performed in front of the 'king', the women's actions may well be projected
differently, more positively.[16] Indeed, it was the presence of persons
resembling kings and nobles which appeared to impart a degree of order and
rationality to the social life of the islands. It was the supposed ruler, for
instance, who appeared to mitigate the native thievery which plagued the
Europeans in their encounters with Polynesian peoples.

These were savages, but human ones, capable of displaying kindness,
generosity, and a degree of grace, in total contrast to the murderers of New
Guinea and Cape York. The Dutch on their part appeared to act in a manner
which departed from the brutality of the Spanish conquistadors in America,
and their actions were seemingly reciprocated: 'In the evening our men
danced with the savages, who were very pleased thereat, being surprised that
we treated them so familiarly and with such kindness. We got to be as free
and easy there as if we had been at home'.[17]

In Futuna, le Maire realized the dream which had been instilled in him
by Quirós. The account of his sojourn in what he believed was the vicinity of
Terra Australis accords well with the words of the Portuguese navigator which
had inspired the expedition. The natives had no apparent religion, living a
carefree life, 'like the birds in the forest'. They had no notion of commerce or
labour; 'the earth of itself gives them all that they need to support life, such
as coker-nuts, obes, bananas and similar products'.[18] The land and its people
recalled the myths of primeval mankind and the Golden Age of the poets.[19] If
the western entrance to the Southland was a wasteland inhabited by bestial
men, the lands lying to the east seemed more like Paradise; Willem Schouten
found them so much to his liking that he declared them to be his personal
Terra Australis.[20]

Dutch Voyages of the 1620s

to the Southland

After disposing of their European rivals in the Indies, the Dutch resumed their efforts to explore the lands discovered by Jansz in 1606. The disastrous wreck of the English vessel the *Trial* in 1622 off the northwest coast of Australia was pointed evidence of the dangers of uncharted waters, and there was always the hope of locating new commercial prospects.

On 21 January 1623 the *Pera* and *Arnhem* set sail for the Southland under the command of Jan Carstensz.[21] Arriving in New Guinea, the explorers became the first Europeans to view the magnificent snow-capped peak of Jaya, whose outline appears on a chart of the *Pera*'s discoveries by Arent Martensz de Leeuw (figure 31).[22] The reception by the natives, however, was in sharp contrast with this idyllic vision. In an encounter with the Papuans at 'Dootslager Rivier' ('Murderers' River') the captain of the *Arnhem*, Dirk

31 Arent Martensz de Leeuw, *Chart of the Discoveries of the* Pera, 1623, MS., Algemeen Rijksarchief, The Hague

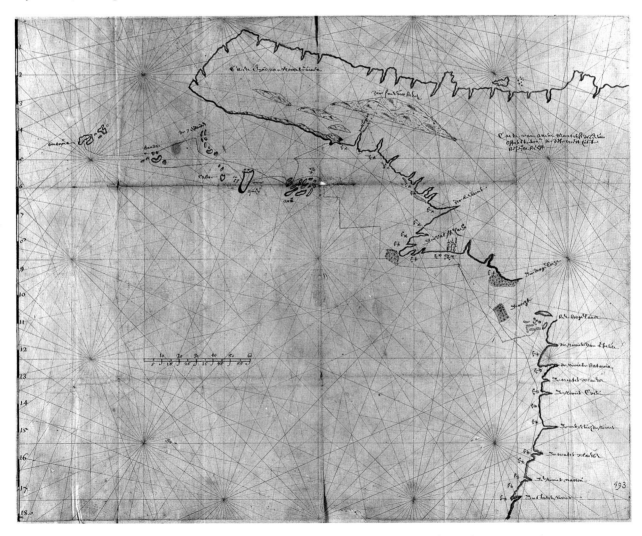

Melisz, and nine crew members were killed; Melisz was succeeded in his post by the second mate of the *Pera*, Willem Joosten van Colster.

Shoals prevented the expedition from entering the Torres Strait; passing to the south, the two ships arrived at Cape York. In April Carstensz became the first white man to examine the Australian interior. He discovered 'a flat, fine country with few trees, and a good soil for planting and sowing, but so far as we could tell utterly destitute of fresh water'. On 26 April the ships began the return voyage to Batavia, with the intention of following the same route; however van Colster sailed directly west in the *Arnhem* across the Gulf of Carpentaria in the belief that this passage constituted the fastest route. In the process he discovered, explored, and charted the region which now bears the name of his vessel – Arnhem Land in the Northern Territory.

Contact with the natives was generally short and violent. This is not surprising as Carstensz had been instructed to kidnap natives so as to train them as interpreters for subsequent voyages. The Aborigines were unable to resist as strenuously as the Papuans did; this may explain why they appear to come off somewhat better in the journal of the voyage: 'They seemed to be less cunning, bold and evil natured than the blacks on the western extremity of New Guinea'. Their weaponry was meagre, although like many 'primitive' people they were adept in its employment. They were armed with 'shields, assagays, and callaways of the length of 1½ fathom, made of light wood and cane, some with fish bones and others with human bones fastened to their tops. They are all very expert in throwing said weapon by means of a piece of wood'.[23] Some of these objects were collected and brought back to Batavia; perhaps they eventually made their way into a Dutch curiosity cabinet.

Carstensz's journal presents a bleak image of Cape York and Arnhem Land:

> The land between 13° and 17°S is an arid and poor tract without any fruit tree or anything useful to man; it is low and monotonous without mountain or hill, wooded in some places with bush and little oily trees; there is little fresh water and what there is can only be collected from pits specially dug; there are also no points or inlets except some bays which are, however, not sheltered against winds from the sea and it extends mainly northeast and southwest all along with muddy and sandy bottoms, with many and different salt rivers which extend inland where their tributaries are overgrown by the dry boughs and foliage of trees. In general the men are barbarians all much alike in build and features, pitch-black and entirely naked, with a knotted net on head and neck for keeping their food in and what they mainly live on (as far as we have seen) were certain roots which they dig out from the earth … Their house or abode we observed in the east monsoons on the beach, here we saw many and different huts made of dry hay; also a great number of dogs, herons, and waterfowl and other wild fowl as also very excellent fish which can easily be caught in a net; they have no knowledge at all of gold, silver, tin, lead and copper; even nutmeg, cloves and paper which had been shown to them several times on the voyage made no impression on them.[24]

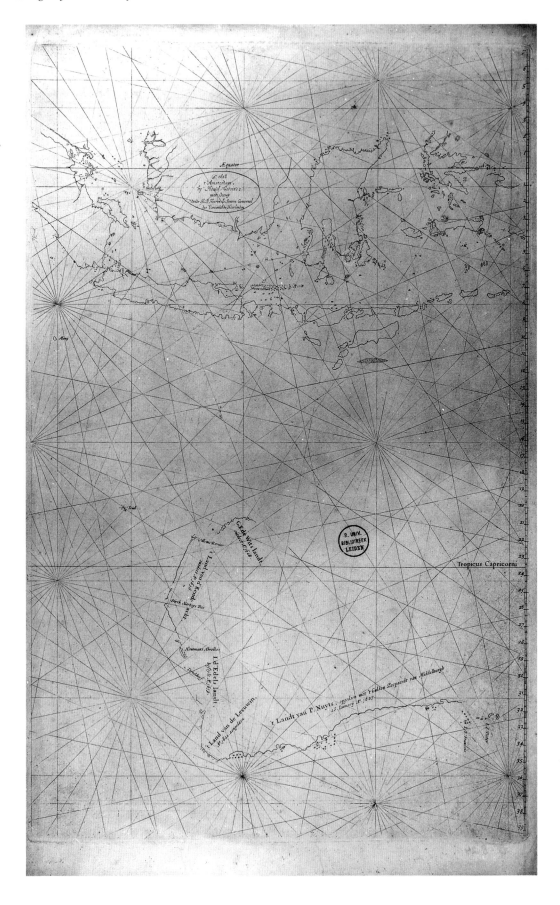

If the Horne Islands inspired visions of the Golden Age, the coasts of
Australia and New Guinea constituted their antithesis. The western part of
the Southland was a barren region. No gold or other precious metals were
to be found there. Nutmeg and cloves – emblematic of Terra Australis in
Plancius's maps thirty years earlier – were unknown. Its inhabitants were
extremely primitive; some were terribly cruel and hostile. By comparison, the
behaviour of the Polynesian 'Southlanders' was extremely benign. The image
of the extensive, vaguely defined region designated as 'Terra Australis/
Southland' was developing along the lines of a bipolarity: bountiful and
welcoming at one extreme, bleak and savage at the other. This vision would
be reinforced by further contacts with the region in the course of the century.

Within five years many of the discoveries made in the course of voyage
of the *Pera* and *Arnhem* could be discerned on printed maps. Information
obtained from the expeditions of Jansz and Carstensz was supplemented by
data acquired as the result of accidental sightings, such as the voyage of the
Leeuwin on the southwest coast (1622) and the *Gulden Zeepard* on the south
coast (including the Great Australian Bight and the Nuyts Archipelago, 1627).
All of the discoveries on the south and west coast were amalgamated in the
revisions made by Hessel Gerritsz to his chart of the Malay Archipelago and
Australia (1618–28) (figure 32),[25] whereas evidence of the *Pera*'s voyage to
Cape York is visible on a number of Dutch maps from the late 1620s and
early 1630s.[26] By 1636, the year in which Antony van Diemen inaugurated a
series of important expeditions in the Southland, the image of the Australian
continent as it appears in modern maps was beginning to emerge.

Antony van Diemen

and the Great Southland:

1636–45

10

The voyages organized by Antony van Diemen during his term of office as governor-general of the Dutch East Indies (1636–45) constituted a significant departure from previous expeditions to the Southland. The explorations sponsored by this remarkable administrator formed part of a systematic, comprehensive attempt to increase the wealth and power of the Netherlands and the Verenigde Oostindische Compagnie (VOC). The two voyages of Abel Tasman to Australia and the South Pacific (1642–43, 1644), the most important of the Dutch expeditions in the region, were an integral part of this program. The maps, charts, and drawings resulting from Tasman's voyages must be understood within the context of van Diemen's geopolitical and economic objectives.

Terra Australis:

the Dutch El Dorado

From the sixteenth century onward the search for Terra Australis had been motivated by economic requirements on the part of Europeans; this was certainly a driving force behind the Spanish and Dutch expeditions we have previously described. The desire for new markets, sources of spices, and precious metals lay behind the voyages of Mendaña, Quirós, Jansz, and Carstensz, and would play an especially important motivating role during the administration of van Diemen as governor-general of the Indies. The quest for gold and silver stimulated a series of interrelated expeditions organized by van Diemen and his associates in the Southland, Asia, and the Pacific. The Dutch quest for El Dorado would have a determining role in the search for Terra Australis in the seventeenth century. The systematic manner in which this program was undertaken underlined the need for extensive, careful graphic records of the areas to be explored.[1]

At the moment in which van Diemen took control of VOC activities in Batavia, a significant imbalance existed between Europe and its trading partners in Asia. Whereas Europeans consistently represented themselves as the dominant force in the world, the image did not entirely correspond to reality. Europe in fact bought more from Asia than it sold, hence the need to pay for goods in precious metals. Apart from the metals seized from Spanish vessels on the open seas, the main source of gold in the Netherlands was Japan; however, the Dutch position as the sole European trading partner of the island empire was a tenuous one. The establishment of a more secure source of precious metals became a principal objective for van Diemen.

The active, intensive search for El Dorado on the part of the VOC in Batavia constituted an exceptional moment in the history of Dutch overseas expansion. The assertive attitude of the new governor-general towards exploration did not coincide with the conservative mentality of the Dutch Republic and the VOC. Although the conquest of the Portuguese Indies brought great wealth to the Netherlands, it did not alter the cautious attitude of the Dutch administrators. The viewpoint from Batavia was very different from that of Amsterdam, where 'efficient accounting and well-organised trade took precedence over risky, capital and labour-intensive undertakings (such as voyages of discovery to "uncivilised" regions, mining activities or the founding of agricultural colonies)'.[2] Antony van Diemen was a protégé of the navigator, entrepreneur and visionary, Hendrik Brouwer (his predecessor as governor-general), and shared Brouwer's enthusiasm for exploration. Like Brouwer, he was a firm believer in the potential wealth of the unexplored southern continent. Together, the two men would initiate a series of voyages which in less than a decade would radically alter the image of the southern world.

Under van Diemen's leadership Batavia became a centre of intense cartographic activity. The daily operations of the office became more systematic; a corps of map-makers was established, as was the position of 'examiner' or supervisor of navigation. Serving within this renovated structure were the men who would play vital roles in the exploration of Australia and the South Pacific. Among the map-makers employed in Batavia was Isaac Gilsemans. A talented calligrapher, cartographer, surveyor, and a competent draughtsman, Gilsemans would serve with distinction in each of these capacities on Tasman's first voyage of 1642–43. From 1634 onwards he had served as clerk to Arnold Gijsels on the latter's tour of inspection in the Moluccas, preparing a series of drawings of the VOC's outposts which have only recently come to light. The position of examiner would be filled by Tasman himself, as well as by his chief navigator in Australasian waters, Frans Jacobsz Visscher, a brilliant cartographer. A hired pilot on Japanese vessels trading on the Gulf of Tonkin in the early 1630s, Visscher transformed the charts created in these waters into highly improved maps of the coasts of China and Indochina, including the islands of Hainan and Taiwan – cartographic documents which would be of great value to van Diemen in his intensive search for precious metals.

The establishment of a centre of graphic documentation in Batavia facilitated the governor-general's efforts to secure new sources of precious metals in Japanese, Australasian, and South Pacific waters. These efforts were initiated in 1636 with the expedition of the *Pool* and *Wesel* to the northwest coast of Australia. Although this venture met with little success, van Diemen was not at all discouraged. In 1637 he sent Tasman in the opposite direction, on a voyage to Tartary (northern China) and Korea. This was a scaled-down version (approved by the VOC in Amsterdam) of a more ambitious undertaking in search of the Gold and Silver Islands believed to exist off the coast of Japan. Notwithstanding the disappointing results, five years later Tasman was placed in command of an expedition to Australia and the South Pacific, which would establish his reputation as one of the greatest explorers of the age.

Abel Tasman in the

Southland 1642–44

The two voyages of Abel Tasman, intended to resolve the issues regarding the nature of the Southland, were an integral part of van Diemen's grand scheme. In addition to a thorough examination of the lands lying to the south and east of the VOC's island empire, Tasman was also expected to find a passage to

Chile across the Pacific within the region of prevailing westerlies. In this manner the governor-general hoped to attack the Spanish possessions on the west coast of America, with their vast gold and silver mines. The conquest of Chile would constitute the crowning achievement of Dutch imperialism, virtually placing all of the oceans of the world under their direct control or influence.

With so much at stake, it is not at all surprising that Tasman's first voyage was prepared with great care. The instructions given to the navigator prior to his departure are important documents for the history of exploration and the visual arts, indispensable for the interpretation of the graphic records of the voyage.

The text, prepared with the assistance of Cornelis Witsen (whose son Nicolaas would assume a significant role in the history of Dutch travel imagery), indicates the great importance given to the role of the draughtsman on the voyage:

> All the lands, islands, points, turnings, inlets, bays, rivers, shoals, banks, sounds, cliffs, rocks etc. which you may meet with and pass, you will duly map out and describe, and also have proper drawings made of their appearance and shape, for which purpose we have ordered an able draftsman to join your expedition.

The same degree of precision in the describing and rendering of coastal features was to be applied to the written and graphic descriptions of the natives and their culture:

> So far as time shall allow, you will diligently strive to gather information concerning the fruits and cattle it [the Southland] produces, their method of building houses, the appearance and shape of the inhabitants, their dress, arms, manners, diet, means of livelihood, religion, mode of government, their wars and the like notable things, more especially if they are kindly or cruelly disposed, showing them various specimens of the commodities you have taken with you for that purpose, so as to learn what materials are found in their country, and what things they are desirous of obtaining from us in return; all of which matters you will carefully note, correctly describe and faithfully set down in drawings.[3]

The nature of the images and accounts of the voyage were affected by the manner and tone of the investigation into the populations to be encountered. The treatment of the natives is explained in detail, providing a clear indication of the care and thought given to the preparations for the expedition, as well as the ideology of its sponsors:

> In landing with small craft extreme caution will everywhere have to be used, seeing that it is well known that the southern regions are peopled with fierce savages, for which reason you will have to be well armed

and to use every prudent precaution, since experience has taught in all parts of the world that barbarian men are no wise to be trusted because they commonly think that the foreigners who so unexpectedly appear before them, have come only to seize their land, which (owing to heedlessness and overconfidence) in the discovery of America occasioned many instances of treacherous slaughter. On which account you will treat with amity and kindness such barbarian men as you shall meet and come to parley with, and connive at small affronts, thefts and the like which they should put upon or commit against our men, lest punishments inflicted should give them a grudge against us; and by shows of kindness gain them over to us, that you may the more readily from them obtain information touching themselves, their country and their circumstances, thus learning whether there is anything profitable to be got or effected ...

You will prudently prevent all manner of insolence and all arbitrary action on the part of our men against the nations discovered, and take good care that no injury be done to them in their houses, gardens, vessels, or their property, their wives etc.; nor shall you carry off any of their inhabitants against their will; should, however, any of them be voluntarily disposed to accompany you, you are at full liberty to bring them hither ...[4]

Although in Tasman's instructions the Southlander has not lost any of his savagery, he has at least acquired a motive for his murderous actions. His violent acts are inspired by the startling appearance of unexpected armed adversaries and the accurate cognition of their malevolent intentions. Kidnapping of the sort perpetrated against the Aborigines by Carstensz and wanton violence were now to be avoided; the thievish behaviour encountered in the Pacific by le Maire was to be tolerated to the greatest extent possible. What van Diemen wished to avoid at all costs was for the natives to bear an eternal grudge against the European such as was imparted to the Indians of Tierra del Fuego by Francis Fletcher. The logic of this viewpoint may have been reinforced by a commonly held belief that the Southlanders were related to the inhabitants of Spanish America. An implied reference to Spanish atrocities in the New World is of course to be expected in a Dutch text of the period; it is apparent, however, that the author is calling into question the actions of his fellow countrymen as well. The preferred model would seem to be that of le Maire's more favourable experiences in Futuna. The benign, even positive image of many of the natives described and depicted in the course of Tasman's voyage coincides with the moderate tone of his instructions.

The drawings and accounts of the expedition indicate that Tasman sought to fulfil the expectations of his patrons by providing a detailed and 'accurate' account of his experiences. It is evident that the author of the drawings in Tasman's journal, Isaac Gilsemans, attempted to render not only the natural features of the land but also the physiognomy and material culture of native people encountered in the course of the voyage. Gilseman's drawings of the natives of New Zealand, Tonga, New Ireland, and the island of Jamna (off the northern coast of New Guinea) are very important as they constitute, to my knowledge, all of the surviving first-hand images of these people executed prior to the eighteenth century. When reproduced in the form of engravings, they would have a significant effect upon the image of the Southland.[5]

Dutch reactions to the people encountered range from very negative (Maoris of New Zealand) to relatively neutral (New Ireland and Jamna) to comparatively positive (Tonga). The pictures and accounts of these meetings were influenced by the length and nature of the meeting. In New Zealand the European–native encounter was short and violent; in New Ireland and Jamna, superficial but benign; in Tonga, more extended and friendly. The voyage reinforced the previous image of the Southland: that of a generally hostile region, populated mainly by brute savages. The northeastern part (Vanuatu, Futuna, Tonga) was altogether different; here was a lush region inhabited by 'soft' primitives living a carefree existence. Through an examination of the Dutch image of the Southland we can trace some of the roots of the utopian myths of the eighteenth century.

Whereas the drawings in Tasman's journal have been attributed to Isaac Gilsemans, it seems probable that the text and its illustrations (especially the coastal profiles) were prepared with the assistance of Frans Jacobsz Visscher, the scientific officer on the expedition. However, Tasman's journal is not the only textual source on the voyage. Another, clearly 'unofficial', account of the voyage was prepared by Hendrik Haalbos, ship's barber and surgeon. Haalbos's description, the first published account of the expedition, was printed in Arnoldus Montanus, *De Nieuwe en Onbekende Weereld* (Amsterdam 1671); an abbreviated and inaccurate English translation appeared at approximately the same time in John Ogilby, *America* (London 1671).[6] Haalbos's account reflects the seaman's point of view far more than the more even-handed, judiciously worded description in the journal; furthermore, it contains a number of additional details which are indispensable for the interpretation of Gilseman's illustrations.

Tasman set sail from Batavia in August 1642 in the *Heemskerck*, a yacht of 120 tons, with a crew of sixty men; accompanying them was the *Zeehaen*, a 200-ton flute (warship used as a transport vessel), commanded by Gerrit Jansz.[7] In a departure from precedent, the expedition sailed southwards to a latitude of 44°S in the Indian Ocean before heading east behind strong westerly winds, eliminating in one stroke a segment of Mercator's Terra Australis. On 24 November the Dutch ships arrived in Tasmania (named Van Diemen's Land by the Dutch), exploring and charting its southeast portion for the next ten days. On 30 November a party of men went ashore to investigate, bringing back samples of vegetables and gum of a high quality. No people were seen; certain evidence of a human presence was reported, however. Two trees had been cut with notches five feet apart, apparently as a means of climbing for the purpose of bird-nesting. The wide distance between these notches led the Dutch to speculate that either the men were very tall or had employed some device to aid their ascent. The possibility of antipodean giants existed, but the prudent Dutch explorers required firm evidence to substantiate any such claims.[8]

Continuing to the east across what is now called the Tasman Sea, the expedition's next landfall occurred on 13 December; Tasman named the newly discovered territory New Zealand, or Statenlandt. The term reflected Tasman's hypothesis that the land was linked to le Maire's Statenland at the southern tip of America.

In Golden Bay on the South Island Tasman had his first encounter with Pacific peoples – a short and bloody affair. With a vocabulary obtained from le Maire in hand, he called out to the Maoris in their canoes, but received no response. He was not surprised, as the men before his eyes bore no resemblance to those encountered twenty-six years earlier in what Tasman, relying upon his predecessor's faulty geography, called the 'Solomons' (actually Futuna). For, unlike the tall, graceful men encountered by le Maire:

> ... these people were (as far as [we] could see) of ordinary height but rough in voice and bones, their colour between brown and yellow, had Black hair right on top of the crown of the head fastened together in style and form like the Japanese at the back of the head but a bit longer and thicker of hair, upon which stood a large thick white feather, their craft were two long Narrow canoes beside each other, over which some planks or other seating was laid, Such that above water one can see through under the vessel their paddles about a large fathom long, narrow and sharp in front; [they] could proceed Speedily with these vessels; their clothing was (So it appeared) some of mats, others Cotton, Some and almost all the upper body naked ...[9]

Having failed at verbal communication, Tasman waved white flags, a sign of peace which was duly ignored. Nor were the Maoris attracted by the knives offered by the Dutch. After the *Zeehaen* launched its small boat in the direction of the shore, the natives finally responded. Paddling their canoes at great speed they attacked the small vessel, killing four crew members, a 'monstrous deed' perpetrated by 'murderers'. In the same way that Carstensz commemorated the bloody massacre on a river in New Guinea, Tasman named the inlet 'Murderers' Bay'. Wishing to avoid further incidents, he set sail to the north.

In Gilsemans's illustration the squat, grim-faced Maoris in their canoe, crudely drawn as they are, appear as suitable perpetrators of the horrifying attack, depicted on a small scale in the middle distance (figure 33). The shape of the canoe correlates with the text, but the feather decorations are conspicuously absent. Other details missing from Tasman's account are supplied by Haalbos, who notes that the Maoris: ' ... wore a square cloak, tied before the throat. In the middle of the canoes, bound together two by two, was the chief, who encouraged the rowers. Among the chiefs stood out a grey man, who came alongside, and called out in a rough and deep voice'.[10]

20 Diego Prado de Tovar, *The Natives of the Bay of San Millán (Southeast New Guinea)*, 1606, watercolour, Archivo General de Simancas

21 Diego Prado de Tovar, *The Natives of the Islands off the southern shores of New Guinea (Torres Strait)*, 1606, watercolour, Archivo General de Simancas

22 Diego Prado de Tovar, *The Natives of the (southwestern) end of New Guinea*, 1606, watercolour, Archivo General de Simancas

37 William Hodges,
Tongatapu or Amsterdam,
1773, watercolour, Rex
Nan Kivell Collection
NK143, National Library
of Australia

33 Isaac Gilsemans,
*Natives of New Zealand
(Golden Bay)*, 1642, MS.,
Algemeen Rijksarchief,
The Hague

Notwithstanding differences in appearance, the Southlanders
encountered by Tasman in New Zealand were considered to be as undesirable
as those encountered in New Guinea and Australia. The diabolical nature of
the Papuans and Aborigines was not thought to be directly related to their
black skin; racism in its modern form did not exist in the seventeenth
century.[11] The principal factor governing the evaluation of native people was
the nature of their reaction to the Dutch. Tasman and his men were not
predisposed to respond negatively to the people they encountered, on the
contrary they were instructed to act in a conciliatory manner. Nevertheless,
the graphic and verbal descriptions of the Maoris – their rough appearance
and harsh voices in particular – were affected by the hostile manner in which
the expedition was received in Golden Bay. The western and southern zones
of the Southland could not have seemed very promising to the Dutch as they
sailed northeast into the Pacific.

A different spirit permeates the pictures and accounts of Tasman's
experiences in Tonga (21–31 January 1643) – an idyllic atmosphere which
corresponds in certain respects to the mood of le Maire's description of
Futuna. Arriving in Tongatapu, the Dutch were warmly received by men who:
'were nude, of brown Colour and somewhat more than ordinary height, two
had long thick hair on the head, the third was shorn short [they] had nothing
but a small quaint cloth in front of their male parts'.[12]

Instead of blows from lances the Dutch received mother-of-pearl fish-hooks in exchange for Chinese mirrors and beads. The natives massed on the shore, waving white flags, which were taken for peace offerings. A small canoe, adorned with such a flag and richly decorated with sea shells and cockles soon arrived, bearing four sturdy men, painted black and wearing large leaves around their necks. The Dutch assumed that this vessel had been sent by the 'king' as a token of friendship. As the ships lay offshore, a host of natives, some of whom wore a mother-of-pearl shell hanging on the breast, brought abundant gifts: bark cloth, a fine large pig, coconuts and yams; many of these were thought to be presents from the 'king' of the island. The Dutch reciprocated for all of this generosity with an ordinary serving dish and a piece of copper wire.

Tasman could not have helped assuming that these people bore some affinity to those encountered by le Maire. He includes a picture of a large canoe in his journal, noting its resemblance to a vessel illustrated in le Maire, although he cannot recall the exact plate number (figure 34).[13] He decided to organize an entertainment along the lines of the concert put on by his predecessor in Futuna:

34 Isaac Gilsemans, *Arrival of Abel Tasman in Tongatapu*, 1643, MS., Algemeen Rijksarchief, The Hague

we got the under-mate of the *Zeehaen* with his Trumpet, and one of their sailors with a violin to come to the ship; [we] had them together with our Trumpeter and one of our sailors who could play on the german flute blow together, and play, which was a surprise to them.[14]

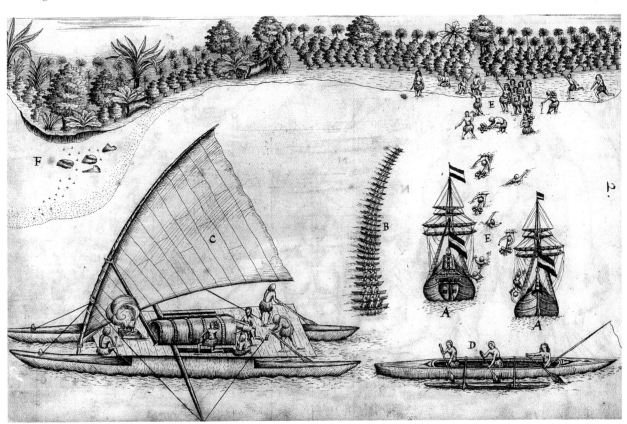

This festivity constituted a prelude to the reception of Tasman and Gerrit Jansz in the *belay* ('royal' dwelling) of the 'chief'. On 23 January the Dutch arrived on the island bearing a white flag, in search of water. They were escorted to the *belay*, where a mat was spread out for them, in preparation for a great feast: ' ... [he] at once had Sweet milk and cream served up, fresh fish, all sorts of fruits which may be obtained there in quantity, [they] did us great honour and friendship ...'.[15]

The 'chief' of Tongatapu proved to be an extremely attentive host, offering water, four live pigs, fowl, coconuts, bananas – in short, all that the Dutch could possibly need or desire. A comparable welcome awaited the expedition upon its arrival the following day at the island of Nomuka. A landing party informed Tasman of its reception:

> on coming to land, [they] had found about 60 to 70 persons Sitting on
> the beach, at which They thought, almost all the menfolk from this
> Island was present, [they] had no weapons but seemed a good peaceful
> people, for [they] found by there many women and children.[16]

The appearance of the Nomukans, their dress and adornments matched those of the inhabitants of Tongatapu, save for the men's hair, which was somewhat shorter and thinner. As for the women Tasman notes only that they ' ... are comparatively Quite as sturdy of body and limbs as the men'.[17] Their behaviour was also comparable – friendly and generous on one hand, immoral on the other: 'This people is exceedingly lascivious wanton and thievish so that argus eyes Are scarcely enough for a person to watch out.'[18] The sexual excesses of the Tongan women are, however, only hinted at by Tasman, whereas thievery was often ignored or played down. For example, no punishment was meted out to a native who stole a pistol from the ship's cabin; the Dutch simply retrieved the object in exchange for a pair of slippers 'Without showing the least annoyance'.[19]

In the course of their excursion to the island in search of water prior to their departure, the Dutch were struck by its idyllic nature. Passing an inland water basin, they saw in the vicinity:

> numbers of plots or gardens in which the beds were made neatly in
> squares, and planted with all sorts of earth-fruits, the banana and other
> fruit trees in many places and almost all standing so straight that it was
> a pleasure to behold, giving from It all round a lovely pleasant aroma
> and odour. So that in this people (who had the form of a man but
> inhuman Morals and customs) also men's ingenuity appeared.[20]

In the midst of the most remote garden ever visited by westerners, Tasman found it difficult to assimilate what he saw. He could not accept the Tongans as wholly human, yet he was struck by their ability to structure natural forms in a harmonious and pleasing manner. The navigator faced similar problems in attempting to describe Tongan civilization for van Diemen and the VOC.

These people, he concluded, had no religious beliefs and no real rulers or government, 'even so they know of wrong and punish the culprits, but this punishment does not happen by law; but by the Innocent'.[21] Polynesian thievery was apparently tempered by a certain self-regulation among the people, not by the orders of a 'king' as le Maire had believed.

Regarding the Polynesian women, Tasman did not associate physical deformity with lasciviousness as did le Maire. He refers to the unchaste behaviour of the people but gives no details, nor does he describe the women as exceedingly ugly or beautiful, merely as rather large. The tone of his remarks corresponds to his role as a presumably neutral observer – a role which he was expected to assume according to his instructions. These constraints did not apply to Haalbos, whose account of an encounter aboard ship in Tongatapu is far more sensational:

> With the men came also many women on shipboard: these were all uncommonly big: but among all stood out two frightful giantesses, one of whom had a moustache: they both grasped the wound-healer Hendrik Haelbos round the neck: each desired fleshly intercourse, whereupon [they] assailed each other with words. All had thick, curly and black hair. Other women felt the sailors shamelessly in the trouser-front, and indicated clearly: that they wanted to have intercourse. The men incited the sailors to such a transgression.[22]

Tasman's description of the incident is much more laconic and reserved, in accordance with the tenor and purpose of his work. He notes only that '18 sturdy men and some womenfolk came on our ship', one of the latter 'by nature had a little beard on the mouth'.[23] The Haalbos narrative functions on an entirely different social and cultural level from the official text. Its author unhesitatingly employs the stereotype of the antipodean giant, scrupulously avoided by Tasman – an image which is in turn conflated with the deformed, lascivious savage woman, analogous to those described in le Maire's account.

Gilsemans's illustrations are compatible with the content and tone of Tasman's text, although certain details can be explained only in reference to Haalbos's account. The events in Tonga are represented on a total of four plates. The first two depict occurrences on Tongatapu, the third and fourth incidents on Nomuka. In the first and third pictures Dutch vessels are contrasted with their native equivalents. The principal events on the island unfold in the second and fourth illustrations in the series; 'typical' examples of Tongan men and women are displayed in large scale, on a kind of plinth, while the narrative scenes are represented in the background. In the second image devoted to Tongatapu a standing couple embrace at the left, whereas a seated pair flank them at the right (figure 35). The man at the far left bears cicatrices on the shoulders and breast – details mentioned only by Haalbos.[24] The ship's barber and surgeon also describes the native's companion at the right, one of the Tongans who welcomed the *Heemskerck* upon its arrival: ' ... a stately man, with a broad black beard: round his neck hung green leaves: [he] proceeded to sit down on the deck with his legs under his body: and

35 Isaac Gilsemans,
Natives of Tongatapu,
1643, MS., Algemeen
Rijksarchief, The Hague

bowed his head several times to the ground'.[25] In his left hand he holds a fly-
whisk, characteristic of the islands. The seated woman at the right, wearing
the type of necklace described by Haalbos, 'made of mother-of-pearl beads,
between which small white shells were threaded',[26] gestures toward the shore.
A group of natives waving white 'peace flags' offer coconuts to the Dutch,
who arrive with their water barrels. In the background the ceremonial *belay*
enclosed by a fence is depicted (marked K in the picture, figure 35), together
with a number of houses. Haalbos notes that among these 'Remarkable houses
in the Unknown South-land', a number 'had an oblong roof of banana or
coconut leaves',[27] a feature clearly visible in the illustration.

On Nomuka a radiant trio of natives, displayed in a comparable
manner, greets the Dutch visitors (figure 36). The woman at the left grasps
the hand of her (disproportionately) small child. The bearded man in the
centre, wearing a mother-of-pearl shell around his neck, offers a bark cloth,
while the woman at the right presents a fish suspended from a pearl fish-
hook. In the background the draughtsman has depicted the inland basin
mentioned in the journal, surrounded by the palm groves which the Dutch
had found so alluring.

A careful examination of the drawings executed by Tasman's
draughtsman indicates that the Dutch, like the British visiting the islands
more than a century later, attempted to record elements of Tongan material
culture. Depictions of necklaces made of pearls and shells, bark cloth and
breast ornaments can be compared with specimens described, drawn, and
collected by Cook and his companions.[28] The houses are not very different in

36 Isaac Gilsemans, *Natives of Nomuka (Tonga)*, 1643, MS., Algemeen Rijksarchief, The Hague

37 William Hodges, *Tongatapu or Amsterdam*, 1773, watercolour, Rex Nan Kivell Collection NK143, National Library of Australia (reproduced in colour following page 76)

form from those rendered by William Hodges and J. R. Forster on Cook's second voyage (figure 37),[29] and the native sailing vessels represented by Gilsemans can be related to those depicted by Hodges in his remarkable washes (figure 38).[30]

38 William Hodges,
*Tonga Tabu or
Amsterdam*, watercolour,
1774, by permission of
the British Library

Furthermore it is probable that certain objects of Polynesian material culture were acquired by the Dutch in Tonga. Haalbos informs us that the natives:

> bartered for some trifles coconuts, bananas, fowls, pigs, mother-of-pearl fish-hooks, stone axes, small seats, heavy clubs full of deep notches, to wound more severely, with a black painted sharp part an arm long, and edged with tough barbs.[31]

Two stone axes in Copenhagen, very similar to those manufactured in Tonga, may bear witness to this exchange of goods (one of these is illustrated as figure 39). The objects, which entered the Royal Danish Kunstkammer in the seventeenth century, are among the very few Pacific artefacts known to have been collected prior to Cook's voyages. Described as 'miners' picks' in an inventory of 1674, the axes may well have been brought back by Tasman as physical evidence of his encounter with the Polynesians.[32]

The mood of the pictures is as striking as the 'ethnographic information' they convey. In contrast to the grim, hostile environment of New Zealand, the Tongan islands constituted a pleasure garden inhabited by a pacific and hospitable race. Although Tasman and his companions were not enthralled by their hosts and surroundings, as Bougainville and Banks were in Tahiti, evidently they regarded the northeastern perimeter of the Southland as its most attractive part. In the descriptions and accounts of the voyage of Abel Tasman (and Jacob le Maire) one can detect the foundations of the myth of the Pacific paradise, derived from and merging with Quirós's utopian vision of Terra Australis.

39 Stone axe, Horne Islands or Tonga, before 1674, Department of Ethnography, The National Museum of Denmark

Upon leaving Tonga, the *Heemskerck* and *Zeehaen* sailed to the northwest in the direction of New Guinea. In early April 1643 they reached the vicinity of Tabar Island off the coast of New Ireland. Brief and superficial in comparison with their visit to Tonga, their encounter with the natives nevertheless inspired an image of historical significance.

The natives who approached the Dutch vessels in their canoes were apparently unarmed and did not harbour any aggressive intentions; Tasman nevertheless remained on his guard lest they engage in any trickery. But after exchanging the meagre goods in their possession – a bit of sago for a bead chain and a belt – the men quickly sped off in their canoes without incident, though not without leaving a certain impression upon the Dutch explorers. Tasman observed that:

> these men are very brown, Yea as black as any kaffir may be the hair of different colour, which thus varies by the spreading of the lime, the face smeared with red paint, apart from the forehead; Some had a white bone through the nose below, which had about the thickness of a little finger, having further nothing on the body than some greenery before their private parts.[33]

Tasman was particularly struck by the appearance of their canoes, noting that they were 'new neatly constructed cut aft and Before in the Form of images, with a wing not very long nor too broad, tapering off sharp in front …'.[34]

In his drawing Gilsemans depicts three men in a canoe, one of whom blows on a conch shell while the others are engaged in rowing and steering the vessel (figure 40). The illustration generally corresponds to Tasman's description, but once again we must refer to Haalbos for certain details, such as the armband worn by the seated oarsman and two curious bow-shaped devices on the vessel. The latter are described as 'oval planks, with a knot in the middle, which [they] used as shields'.[35] Haalbos did not guess the real purpose of these implements, which are actually 'propellers' suspended in the water to attract and catch sharks.[36] Interestingly, Haalbos describes a nearly identical fishing practice among the Tabar Islanders without realizing that the 'shields' actually performed a similar function.[37]

Perhaps the greatest challenge to Gilsemans's ability as a draughtsman was the rendering of the sculptures decorating the bow and stern of the canoe – 'elegant figures' in Haalbos's words. This must be the earliest attempt to replicate the art of New Ireland, two and a half centuries prior to its 'discovery' by Europeans searching for the 'primitive'. Gilsemans, of course, was not encumbered by any modern notions of primitivism. His image is a curious amalgam. Beneath a curved crest – roughly equivalent to the actual configuration of such objects – he has rendered something resembling the Alpine devil masks of Austria and Switzerland.[38] Unable to replicate with precision the strange and complex form, he may have incorporated familiar aesthetic elements from his own part of the world.

Tasman continued west along the northern coast of New Guinea, adding depictions of the natives of Jamna Island (present-day Irian Jaya) to his

40 Isaac Gilsemans, *Natives of Tabar Island in a Canoe*, 1643, MS., Algemeen Rijksarchief, The Hague

collection of images; in this instance the text of the journal has very little to say, and we must rely upon Haalbos for explanatory details.[39] The expedition arrived in Batavia in June 1643 after a voyage of ten months. Although Tasman demonstrated his considerable abilities as a seaman, van Diemen was not satisfied with the results of the expedition. No sources of gold or spices were discovered. The geographical limits of the Southland could now be grasped to a greater extent than before, and the feasibility of an eastward passage to Chile appeared to be confirmed, but the nature of the austral lands and their inhabitants remained largely unknown. Van Diemen was in fact highly critical of Tasman, writing to his superiors that the explorer 'has not made many investigations regarding the situations nor form and nature of the discovered lands and peoples, but has in principle left everything to a more inquisitive successor'.[40]

Van Diemen's comments are perhaps more of a reflection on his own high standards and ambitions than on any deficiencies on the part of Tasman, Visscher, or Gilsemans. The type of full-scale, systematic investigation which he envisaged was beyond the customary limits imposed upon voyages sponsored by the VOC. In any case he retained sufficient faith in Tasman's abilities to place him in command of a second expedition the following year, consisting of the yachts *Limmen* and *Zeemeuw*, the galliot *de Bracq*, and 111 men. The voyage had a twofold stated purpose: first, to determine if a passage existed between the Southland and New Guinea, second, to ascertain whether it was possible to sail from the Gulf of Carpentaria to Van Diemen's Land.

Undoubtedly the expedition also formed part of van Diemen's continuing search for precious metals. In 1643 Maarten Gerritsz de Vries and his crew sailed from Batavia to Tartary in pursuit of this aim, becoming 'the first Europeans to visit the east coast of Hokkaido, part of Sakhalin and some of the Kuril Islands'.[41]

Unfortunately, Tasman had no more success than Jansz or Carstensz had had in locating the Torres Strait, therefore leaving the question of the

41   Joan Blaeu, *World Map*, 1645-46, engraving, Maritiem Museum 'Prins Hendrik', Rotterdam

relationship between New Guinea and Australia unresolved. He explored the Gulf of Carpentaria, demonstrating to everyone's satisfaction that no passage to Tasmania existed, sailing along the northwest coast prior to returning to Batavia. No log-book of the voyage survives, but its route is outlined in the so-called Bonaparte map in the Mitchell Library, Sydney.[42] In spite of the lack of documentary evidence we can be certain that Tasman's impression of the northwest part of the Southland did not alter the prevailing negative view

of the region. Van Diemen reported to the directors of the VOC that the expedition 'found nothing profitable, only poor, naked people walking along the beaches, without rice or many fruits, very poor and bad-tempered in many places'.[43]

The results of Tasman's voyages soon became widely known to the European public through a series of magnificent maps and globes celebrating the triumph of the Netherlands as a great power. The first of these, executed in 1645–46 by Joan Blaeu, the cartographer of the VOC, was a revised version of the great map his father Willem had published twenty-seven years earlier. Only one copy of Joan Blaeu's visual encyclopedia survives, preserved in a damaged state in the Maritiem Museum 'Prins Hendrik', Rotterdam (figure 41).[44] Around its borders are portraits of the peoples of the world and an illustrated text replete with information on geography, ethnography, and natural history; in the segment devoted to the Dutch East Indies one encounters images of two creatures often identified with the Southland – an emu and a bird of paradise. In the southeast portion of the eastern hemisphere, a relatively complete outline of the western portion of Australia appears for the first time, with the designation *Nova Hollandia* ('New Holland').

Two years later the results of Tasman's discoveries would reappear on a world map by Blaeu engraved on twenty copper plates and commemorating the Peace of Munster (1648), marking the zenith of Dutch sea-power.[45] Reproduced on maps, atlases, and globes, cartographic images based upon this new vision of the world would be widely disseminated. Gilsemans's pictures of the Southland would, however, remain unpublished for sixty years. It would be over two decades before the appearance of the first published description of the expedition of 1642–43, and a full account based upon Tasman's journal did not appear in print for more than eighty years after the voyage.

The Westindische Compagnie,
Chile and the
Southern Continent

While the VOC explored the southern continent from its base in the East Indies, a parallel effort was undertaken by its sister company, the Westindische Compagnie, or Dutch West India Company (WIC), in the western hemisphere. Once again the search for precious metals constituted a primary motivation. The protagonist of this saga was van Diemen's mentor, Hendrik Brouwer, a man who, like Quirós, was obsessed with Terra Australis.

The end result of this westward probe would be the further diminution of the map of Magellanica.[46]

In 1629 an expedition led by Maarten Valck and Johannes van Walbeeck was launched with the intention of establishing a Dutch base on the Chilean coast and to explore Terra Australis. As a result of colonial wars between the Netherlands and Portugal this expedition did not get beyond Brazil. Thirteen years later, in 1642, at roughly the same moment in which Tasman set off for Van Diemen's Land, the WIC revived the idea of a thrust into the Spanish Pacific coast. Hendrik Brouwer assumed command of the expedition with the intention of pursuing his dream of finding the great

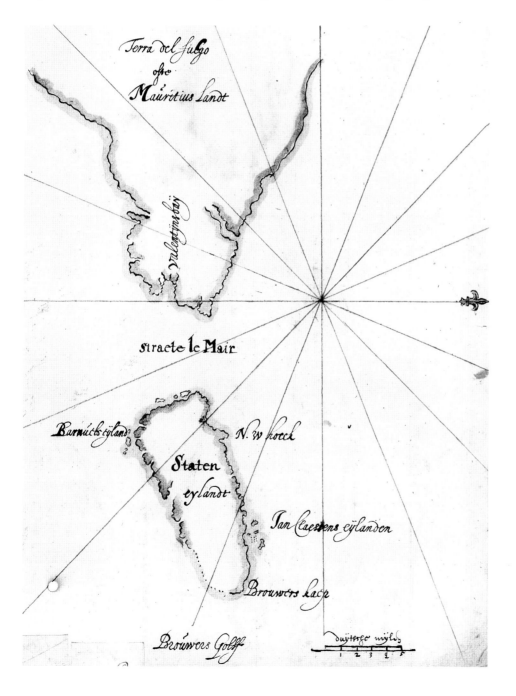

42 *Chart of Brouwers Golf (Drake Passage) and Stateneiland, 1643, MS., Algemeen Rijksarchief, The Hague*

southern continent. The Dutch succeeded in establishing a fort on the Chilean coast, but the death of Brouwer brought an end to Dutch hopes of challenging Spanish dominance in the eastern Pacific shores. The ill-fated venture also marked the final attempt to locate the rich austral world believed to lie beyond the west coast of South America.

Cartographic documents derived from this expedition are eloquent testimony to the erosion of Magellanica. In 1616 Jacob le Maire had discovered a passage south of Tierra del Fuego, the Le Maire Strait. The land to the south of this body of water was designated as the Statenland; it was this imagined portion of Terra Australis which, according to Tasman, was probably linked to New Zealand. Brouwer's investigation demonstrated that le Maire's Statenland was in fact Staten Island, a correction made directly on the map recording the results of the former's voyage (figure 42).[47] Mercator's Terra Australis, shifted even further south, began to lose coherence. In late seventeenth-century maps it appears as a broken coastline; the only portion remaining fully intact is the section below Africa (figure 43).[48] For the next 125 years, geographers and explorers searching for Terra Australis concentrated on the area consisting of what is known as Australia, New Guinea, New Zealand, Vanuatu and neighbouring islands.

The deaths of Brouwer, in 1643, and of van Diemen, two years later, marked the disappearance of the men who had provided the principal stimulus for the search for Terra Australis on the part of the Dutch Indies

43 Nicholas Sanson, *World Map*, engraving, 1678, Algemeen Rijksarchief, The Hague

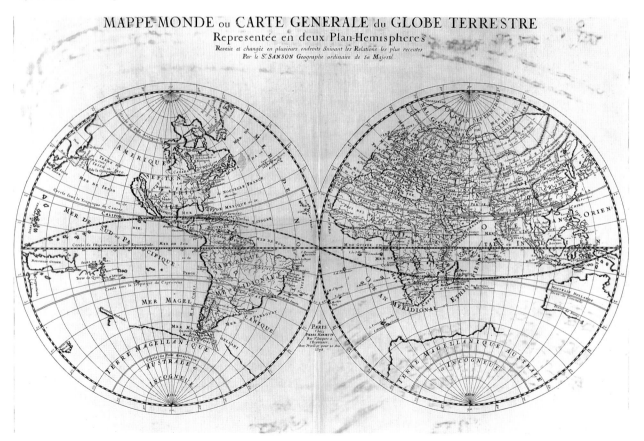

companies. After 1645 the VOC and WIC were reluctant to undertake any risky ventures, preferring to concentrate on trade. The WIC abandoned all efforts in this direction, while the Tasman voyages constituted the end of deliberate Australian exploration on the part of the VOC for fifty years.

The failures of the Tasman voyages should not detract from their importance for the history of scientific voyages and the role played by artists in these undertakings. Gilsemans's drawings are evidence of the significance of art in Dutch expansion and exploration in the seventeenth century. Their existence provided a precedent for the employment of artists on Cook's voyages of the eighteenth century. The paths connecting manifestations of the same phenomenon in the Netherlands and Britain over the course of more than a century are circuitous, however; we should not be disappointed if we cannot trace a progressive triumph of art in the service of science.

Art and the Dutch Trading Companies

11

The early images of the Southland and its inhabitants pertain to a larger context of art and exploration in the United Provinces during the seventeenth and eighteenth centuries. It should be noted at once that large-scale scientific expeditions sponsored by the state and accompanied by artists were not undertaken in the Netherlands during this period. Nevertheless, artists and draughtsmen were present in many distant lands under the control or influence of the Verenigde Oostindische Compagnie (VOC) and the Westindische Compagnie (WIC): Brazil, Surinam, New Amsterdam (New

York), West and South Africa, India, China, Japan, Sri Lanka, Malaya, the East Indies.[1] In addition to preparatory drawings for maps and atlases, they executed portraits of the governors of the Indies, and a large number of plant and animal studies. Art played a role in the entire enterprise of trade and colonization, a role that was essentially propagandistic and diplomatic. Paintings, particularly those representing important victories such as the Dutch triumph over Spain at Gibraltar (figure 44), were sold or given to Eastern rulers as symbols of the might of the VOC. Sumptuously decorated maps, globes, and prints were likewise highly valued as diplomatic gifts.

Complementing this artistic practice was the collection and presentation of 'rarities' – ethnographic artefacts, works of art, plant and animal specimens from all parts of the trading empire. These objects found their way into the private museums of trading companies, artists and writers, merchants, physicians, and the nobility in the Netherlands and throughout Europe.[2] Specimens were valued, not only for the scientific information they may have provided, but also for their rarity, and the prestige they imparted to their owners (figure 45).[3] Drawings, sketches, and paintings reproducing these exotic subjects became rarities in their own right, imbued with the mystery and fascination of the specimen itself.

The account of the reception given in 1638 by the city of Amsterdam to the exiled queen of France, Marie de' Medici, provides a vivid impression of the manner in which the Dutch sought to display and represent their riches.[4] The queen was escorted at midday into the banquet hall of the VOC directors. Here hung rare Chinese and Japanese paintings, the imposing images of the Dutch fortress of Batavia, the castle of Osaka in Japan, and views of the principal Company factories in the Moluccas, Japan, and the Chinese coast. An extraordinary collection of exotica – lances, spears, axes,

44 Adam Willaerts, *The Defeat of the Spaniards at Gibraltar*, 1607, oil on canvas, Rijksmuseum–Stichting, Amsterdam

45 Hendrik Goltzius,
*The Shell Collector Jan
Govertson (1545-1617)*,
1600, oil on canvas,
Museum Boymans–van
Beuningen, Rotterdam
(reproduced in colour
following page 108)

and interlocking shields – lined the walls. In the reception hall a great feast
was set out for the queen, prepared with an array of spices and foods brought
to Amsterdam by the VOC from the Near East, Far East, and India, served on
splendid porcelain plates imported by the Company from China.

In the course of the reception of Marie de' Medici at the East India
House the Company projected its power and strength in the form of a great
baroque spectacle, a feast for the senses. The edifice providing the setting for
this event combined the features of an office and warehouse with those of a
museum and curiosity cabinet.[5] It housed within its walls a vast collection
of visual information – maps, charts and drawings – serving the Company's
interests both as practical instruments of navigation and as propaganda.

At the same time it must be remembered that the Dutch Indies companies, east and west, were not scientific societies and in general did not sponsor expeditions.[6] When they did so, it was purely for economic reasons, as the study of topography, plants, animals, and human cultures played a particular role in advancing their commercial interests. No central organization comparable to the British Royal Society, the patron of the Cook voyages, existed in the Netherlands at the time. Scientific investigations involving the participation of artists were generally private initiatives; often the companies did not especially encourage the collecting zeal of amateurs. Patrons were generally aristocrats and public officials, men of considerable private means. The most important of these in terms of the visual arts was Count Johan Maurits van Nassau-Siegen, governor of the Dutch colony in Brazil from 1637 to 1645. Maurits employed a team of talented artists to produce a comprehensive pictorial record of Brazilian natural history, topography, and ethnography, complementing a significant collection of specimens and artefacts. Whereas no other individual in the Netherlands had the means to create a museum of comparable magnitude, a number of amateurs with important contacts within the VOC and WIC were able to assemble large collections. In the second half of the century the most influential of these patrons and collectors was Nicolaas Witsen, whose father Cornelis, as previously noted, assisted in the preparation of Tasman's instructions. Nicolaas shared his father's great interest in the Southland, and it was on his behalf that the final large-scale Dutch expedition to Australia was undertaken: the voyage of Willem de Vlamingh (1696–97).

The Brazilian Rarities
of Johan Maurits

Certainly the most significant Dutch overseas enterprise from the point of view of the arts was the administration of Count Johan Maurits van Nassau-Siegen as governor of Brazil on behalf of the WIC (1637–45) (figure 46).[7] Under his direction the naturalists Georg Marcgraf and Willem Piso, together with the artists Frans Post and Albert Eckhout, produced a visual survey of Brazil which remained unequalled until the nineteenth century. Post's scenic landscapes, replete with native vegetation and accurate renderings of exotic terrain, incorporate all of the characteristics of the 'typical' landscape described by Bernard Smith (figure 47), whereas the paintings and drawings of Eckhout set new standards in the depiction of exotic plants and animals as

well as non-European people (figures 48, 49, 50). Woodcuts based upon
Eckhout's studies illustrated the *Historia naturalis Brasiliae* of Piso and
Marcgraf (Leiden 1648), the standard work on Brazilian natural history
for nearly two centuries. Joseph Banks, who carried a copy aboard the
Endeavour, noted in the course of the ship's stopover in Brazil that no one
interested in botany had visited the country subsequent to the researches of
these two scholars.[8]

In certain respects Maurits and van Diemen had similar goals: the
visual documentation of unknown or little known natural and human
environments. However, whereas van Diemen would have probably wished to
employ the services of an artist with more ability than Isaac Gilsemans, he
had to be satisfied with what was possible. It would have been difficult to

47 Frans Post, *The São Francisco River and Fort Maurits, Brazil*, 1638, oil on canvas, Musée du Louvre, Paris

48 Albert Eckhout, *Still Life with Pineapple, Passionfruit, and other Fruits*, ca. 1642, oil on canvas, Department of Ethnography, The National Museum of Denmark, Copenhagen

49 Albert Eckhout,
Tupi Woman with Child,
1641, oil on canvas,
Department of
Ethnography, The
National Museum of
Denmark, Copenhagen

50 Albert Eckhout,
Tarairiu Woman, 1641,
oil on canvas, Department
of Ethnography, The
National Museum of
Denmark, Copenhagen

convince a painter of the stature of Post or Eckhout to sail with Tasman into possible, even probable oblivion. By contrast, whereas Brazil could not be compared with the more tranquil towns and countryside of the Netherlands, it would have appeared more attractive than the uncharted edge of the known world. Maurits's Brazilian endeavour was an enterprise of the first magnitude in scientific and artistic terms, even though it does not really compare to Tasman's venture in terms of a voyage of exploration.

In Brazil Maurits established what may be described as a study centre, comprising a zoo, astronomical observatory, botanical garden, and painting gallery. Although Batavia may have provided some of the same facilities, the VOC governors did not generally have the desire and certainly not the means to engage in a comparable undertaking (even though a number of them did so on a smaller scale). The works of art and scientific studies commissioned by Maurits were engendered by a particular sort of princely patronage that was not possible in the more tightly organized commercial empire of the VOC.

Having said this, we may still find some analogies between Gilsemans's studies of Pacific islanders and Albert Eckhout's full-length portraits of Brazilian Indians (National Museum, Copenhagen). Both present isolated 'typical' examples of native peoples with characteristic elements of dress, ornament, and so on, set against a landscape background which elucidates the meaning or context of the figures. These nearly contemporary works function, on the level of figuration, as expressions of what Svetlana Alpers has described as the 'mapping impulse' in Dutch art of the period.[9] Alpers's term would apply more precisely to Gilsemans's drawings, in which elements of cartographic and pictorial representation are compressed within the same space.

On another level, beyond the purely figurative, Eckhout's Indian portraits comprise part of a cycle of works representing the non-white social structure upon which the Dutch founded their Atlantic empire: black Africans, mestizos and mulattos, as well as the indigenous people of Brazil. They are not purely scientific documents, even if they may convey precious anthropological, botanical, and zoological information. Maurits commissioned these extraordinary works as pictorial embodiments of the system he controlled from his Vrijburg palace in present-day Recife, where the pictures were probably exhibited.

As Ernst van den Boogaart has observed, the Indian portraits are best understood in the context of the entire cycle, as reflections of Dutch attitudes towards these 'less-civilized' people.[10] The painting of a Tupi woman and child, with a banana plant in the right foreground and a plantation in the distance (figure 49), projects a mood of order and serenity (perhaps analogous to the sentiments evoked by Gilsemans's relatively sympathetic pictures of Tongans). These savages have a certain potential to be civilized, to be controlled for the benefit of Europeans. The Tarairiu, on the other hand, are portrayed as irredeemably wild cannibals, in an uncultivated landscape accompanied by serpents (figure 50). Like the Papuans and Maoris, they would remain outside the perimeter of the civilized world.

45 Hendrik Goltzius,
*The Shell Collector Jan
Govertson (1545-1617),*
1600, oil on canvas,
Museum Boymans–van
Beuningen, Rotterdam

52 *Capture of Loki on
Ceram by Arnold de
Vlamingh*, ca. 1670,
watercolour, *Atlas van der
Hem*, Österreichische
Nationalbibliothek,
Vienna

59 Louis Renard after
Samuel Fallours, *The
Great Table Fish*, 1718,
hand-coloured engraving
from *Poissons, Ecrevisses
et Crabes …*

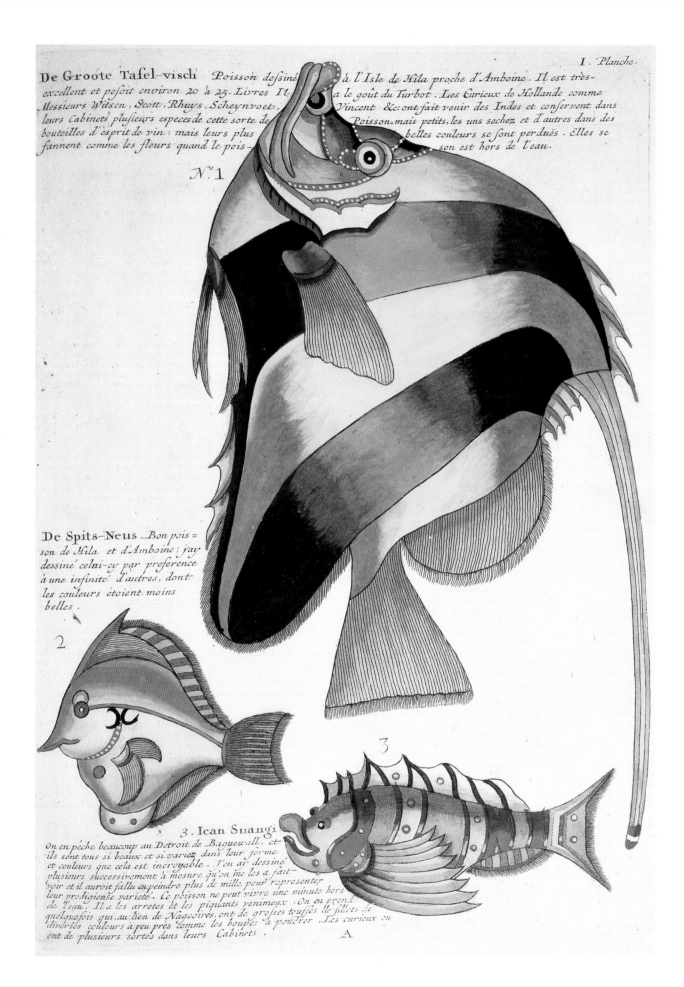

De Groote Tafel-visch Poisson dessiné à l'Isle de Hila proche d'Amboine. Il est très-excellent et pesoit environ 20 à 25 Livres Il a le goût du Turbot. Les Curieux de Hollande comme Messieurs Witsen, Scott, Rhuys, Scheynvoet, Vincent &c: ont fait venir des Indes et conservent dans leurs Cabinets plusieurs especes de cette sorte de Poisson, mais petits, les uns sechez, et d'autres dans des bouteilles d'esprit de vin: mais leurs plus belles couleurs se sont perduës. Elles se fannent comme les fleurs quand le pois- son est hors de l'eau.

N°. 1

De Spits–Neus . Bon pois = son de Hila et d'Amboine; j'ay dessiné celui-cy par preference à une infinité d'autres, dont les couleurs étoient moins belles.

2

3

3. **Ican Suangi**

On en péche beaucoup au Detroit de Baguewall, et ils sont tous si beaux et si variez dans leur forme et couleurs que cela est incroyable. J'en ai dessiné plusieurs successivement à mesure qu'on me les a fait voir et il auroit fallu en peindre plus de mille pour representer leur prodigieuse varieté. Ce poisson ne peut vivre une minute hors de l'eau. Il a les arretes et les piquants venimeux. On en prend quelquefois qui au lieu de Nageoires, ont de grosses touffes de fillets de diverses couleurs à peu près comme les houpes à poudrer. Les curieux en ont de plusieurs sortes dans leurs Cabinets.

A

62 Godfrey Kneller,
Cornelis de Bruijn, ca.
1700, oil on canvas,
Rijksmuseum–Stichting,
Amsterdam

The imposing dimensions of Eckhout's life-size portraits imbue the images with a particular social meaning which sets them apart from other forms of figuration. As unique, irreplaceable and monumental works, they are in effect equivalent to the rarities they represent, embodying the magnificence and prestige of their patron and owner. As such, they constituted valuable objects, which could be sold or presented as gifts for political or economic purposes. At the same time, Eckhout's direct observations of tropical Brazil might in turn serve as a rich source material for decorations on an even larger scale. Clearly, these works functioned on different social and artistic levels simultaneously. Johan Maurits, a great patron of art and science, was at the same time extremely conscious of the multiple social functions of art within his own courtly circle.

In 1654 twenty-six paintings by Eckhout of Africans and Brazilians, together with his still-lifes of tropical fruits, were presented to King Frederick III of Denmark. In his letter of presentation Johan Maurits emphasized the unique character of the pictures as well as their potential value as sources for other works.[11] At the end of his life, under financial duress, Maurits offered a large quantity of plant, animal, ethnographic and landscape studies, together with some artefacts, to the king of France, Louis XIV.[12] The presentation took place in 1678–79 against the background of the peace negotiations between France and the Netherlands at Nijmegen. In his letter to the French foreign minister, the Marquis de Pomponne, the count emphasizes the potential value of his collection of objects and images for the court of Versailles:

> The said *rarities* portray all of Brazil so that one may know the nation and the inhabitants of the country, the four-legged animals, the birds, fish, fruits and herbs – all life size – as well as the situation of the country, towns and fortresses, in perspective. From these portrayals one can design a tapestry to decorate a great hall or gallery, which would constitute *a very rare thing, not found anywhere in the world*. [emphasis added][13]

In his entreaty addressed to the French court Maurits reveals his awareness of the dual nature of the works in his collection: conveyors of very specific information, they also function on the level of decoration and artifice. This duality of perception and knowledge was echoed at the court of Versailles. On the occasion of the presentation, certain members of the French court expressed scepticism regarding the existence of the animals represented by Maurits's artists. The king's brother was able to resolve all questions by reading appropriate descriptions from a text supplied with the gift: a French translation of Piso and Marcgraf's *Historia naturalis Brasiliae*. 'Puisque le prins Mauris le dit', no further doubts were expressed.[14]

We may assume that copies of the original text would have been available in the royal library, and the king, an important patron of the sciences, may well have been able to call upon the services of one of his own naturalists to explain the works. The environment of the Versailles courtier was, however, somewhat removed from the gardens and zoos where Louis XIV's botanists and zoologists investigated specimens brought from overseas. The 'Indes', a set of Gobelin tapestries inspired by the Maurits collection, reflect the dual nature of the court (figure 51).[15] Carefully observed aspects of the Brazilian natural environment are set into a dense exotic world, blending elements from the tropical zones east and west. The only possible precedent for such a display of natural history and exotica which comes to mind would have been the lost pictures of New World subjects in the Escorial. In the 'Indes' an imaginary vision of a tropical Utopia is constructed from the most accurate images of the non-European environment which had ever been produced. In the highest levels of seventeenth-century court culture, art and scientific exploration had become intertwined in an extraordinarily complex manner.

51 After Albert Eckhout, *L'Elephant ou le Cheval Isabelle*, 1689, tapestry, Mobilier Nationale, Paris

The Dutch East India Company
and the Visual Arts

Although nothing on the scale of the Maurits collection and its legacy emerged from Dutch expansion in the East, the works of art related to the enterprises of the VOC are of considerable interest. Of these, undoubtedly the most magnificent is the *Atlas van der Hem*, or *Secret Atlas* of the VOC, in the National Library, Vienna.[16] We have already had occasion to mention this remarkable work, within which are preserved some the most precious cartographic documents of Australia's discovery. The *Atlas van der Hem* (named after its original owner, the wealthy lawyer Laurens van der Hem) is, however, more than a collection of maps. Its folio leaves contain a systematic pictorial inventory of all of the islands, cities and towns associated with Dutch commercial interests, rendered in explicit detail and brilliant, beautiful colours.

The *Atlas van der Hem* celebrates the power of the Dutch Indies empire at its apogee. Images of military campaigns based on first-hand drawings, such as the plate depicting the destruction of the Moluccan fortress of Loki (Ceram) by Arnold de Vlamingh in 1652, indicate the fate of those who would defy the VOC's might. The carefully rendered Indonesian vessels offshore, bearing Dutch flags, extol the advantages of indigenous participation in these campaigns of subjugation (figure 52).[17] By contrast, the tranquil, idyllic image of the eastern portion of the island of Ternate (figure 53) may indicate the benefits of submitting to superior force. The lands of the East, including New Holland (represented in the atlas in vol. 41, pl. 32, recording Tasman's

52 *Capture of Loki on Ceram by Arnold de Vlamingh*, ca. 1670, watercolour, *Atlas van der Hem*, Österreichische Nationalbibliothek, Vienna (reproduced in colour following page 108)

53 *Ternate viewed from the East*, ca. 1670, watercolour, *Atlas van der Hem*, Österreichische Nationalbibliothek, Vienna

discoveries) are depicted as gleaming jewels in the hands of the Netherlands. This vision was accessible only to the higher echelons of society. The atlas was never completely published, and of course the engraved maps and views that did appear could not compare with the superbly coloured manuscript plates now in Vienna. The impact of the work upon the European aristocracy is suggested by the following entry from the journal of Cosimo III de' Medici's visit to Amsterdam in 1668:

> When Blaeu arrived he (Cosimo) wanted to see in the house of the lawyer van der Hem a cabinet with a grand collection of drawings of various cities, coasts and places of the Indies, excellently miniatured, and other maps, both universal and particular, made by hand, with every sort of exquisiteness imaginable.[18]

While the *Atlas van der Hem* constitutes the finest work produced directly under the auspices of the VOC, it represents only one aspect of the Company's relationship with the visual arts, even though this relationship was in some manner an indirect one. Although the interests of the VOC were economic and not scientific or artistic, many scientists and draughtsmen working within its infrastructure collected specimens and produced an enormous quantity of natural history studies in the most remote parts of the Dutch empire.[19] The binary classification system created by Linnaeus, the framework for Cook's scientists and artists, was based upon the massive amounts of data and imagery collected and produced in the Netherlands overseas territories.[20]

Although the VOC had no interest in science for its own sake, and viewed with a certain displeasure the research and collecting undertaken by amateurs, the nature of its commercial undertakings necessitated some involvement in scientific investigation. Artists' services were essential for the execution of these tasks, just as they were required for the proper documentation of coastlines and, ideally, of native dress, weaponry, customs and religious practices.

In the first place the survival of Dutch merchants and seamen in tropical areas required information on medicines to combat diseases endemic to these regions. To facilitate research, Company officials recorded their observations on the plants and animals that were potentially useful for the preparation of medicines. Among the earliest of these naturalists working on behalf of the VOC was Jacobus Bontius (1592–1631), personal physician to Jan Pieterszoon Coen, governor-general in Batavia. His investigations laid the groundwork for the study of tropical medicine and served as a source of inspiration for the Brazilian researches of Piso and Marcgraf.[21]

54 Georg Everhard Rumphius, *Caricature plant (New Guinea)*, watercolour, MS., *Herbarium Amboinense*, ca. 1692, Bibliotheek der Rijkuniversiteit, Leiden, (MS. BPL 311 VI, f. 130r)

In the course of the second half of the century, the growth of VOC power and influence in Asia and the increase in European colonization led to intensified study of commercial crops. These were essential for participation in Asian regional markets as well as for the sustenance of European populations in the region. The Company developed a keen interest in any plants or crops, including coffee and tea, which could be exploited to commercial advantage. A number of the officials engaged in these research tasks achieved renown through their profusely illustrated scholarly publications and, as a result of their books and correspondence, became integrated into the worldwide Republic of Letters of the seventeenth and eighteenth centuries. Indeed, it was through the exchange of information, specimens, and drawings among scholars throughout the world, and not only through scientific voyages, that information regarding the natural history of remote regions was accumulated prior to the nineteenth century. The great expeditions of the eighteenth century were inspired by, and predicated upon this international research.

55 H. A. van Rheede tot Drakenstein, *Papaya*, engraving from *Hortus Indicus Malabaricus* (1678-1703), Library of the Royal Botanic Gardens, Sydney

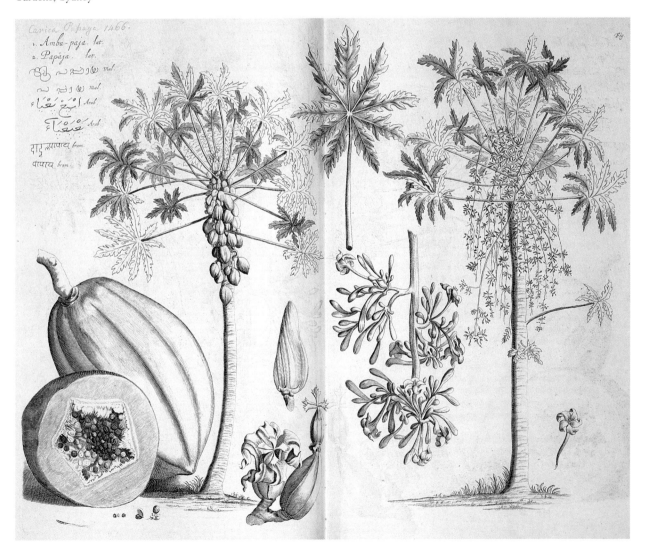

Among the more accomplished of these Company servants was Georg Everhard Rumphius, a merchant in Ambon, whose studies were supported by Johannes Camphuis, governor-general in Batavia.[22] In the course of his research Rumphius described and illustrated nearly one thousand tropical plants (figure 54). These were published after a delay of many years in the *Herbarium Amboinense*, another reference volume in Banks's library on the *Endeavour*. Rumphius's *Amboinsche Rariteitkamer* (1705) became a basic reference work for tropical shell collectors; his own collection was acquired by Cosimo III de' Medici. In India the commissioner-general Hendrik Adriaan van Rheede tot Drakenstein worked in collaboration with local authorities and draughtsmen to produce a superbly illustrated botanical work, the *Hortus Indicus Malabaricus* (1678–1703), filled with exuberant still-lifes of tropical fruit (figure 55).[23] A half-century later, Joan Gideon Loten, Dutch governor of Ceylon (1752–57), a Fellow of the Royal Society, commissioned an extensive series of exquisite watercolour drawings of birds from the painter Peter de Bevere (figure 56). Many of these pictures were acquired by Joseph Banks

56 **(left)** Peter de Bevere, *Red Lory from the Islands adjacent to Banda*, ca. 1753-57, watercolour, Department of Natural History, copyright British Museum

57 **(right)** Engelbert Kaempfer, *Tiger Lily*, ca. 1690, pen and dark brown ink, by permission of British Library

and were copied by Sydney Parkinson, natural history painter on the *Endeavour*, shortly before the vessel's departure for the Pacific.[24] In the VOC factory of Deshima in Nagasaki harbour, the surgeon Engelbert Kaempfer wrote a number of very important works on Japanese history, ethnography, and flora. His *Amoenitatum exoticarum politico-physico* (first edition, Lemgo 1712), illustrated with engravings after his own extremely delicate, refined drawings (figure 57) would be republished by Banks in 1791.[25] At the Cape of Good Hope, gateway to the Dutch East Indies, a flourishing botanical garden was established in the seventeenth century. From this outpost the VOC governor, Simon van der Stel, launched expeditions into the interior to survey the region's natural resources. On one of these journeys, to Namaqualand (1685), the apothecary Hendrik Claudius executed a series of drawings representing African plants and animals (figure 58).[26]

Our brief survey can only give a general indication of the important role of scientific investigation and illustration in the Dutch East Indies during the seventeenth and eighteenth centuries. The drawings and engravings executed in these remote regions are indicative of intense curiosity and careful observation, but also reflect the amazement which these newly discovered species must have evoked. Perhaps the most fascinating of all of the life forms encountered for the first time in the Dutch East Indies were the multicoloured species of tropical marine life. An extensive series of drawings of marine life, executed in intense, brilliant colours, permits us to appreciate the impact of the initial encounter with these seemingly bizarre creatures. The studies were executed in Ambon by Samuel Fallours between 1703 and 1712 on behalf of a number of prominent VOC officials. Shortly thereafter they were transformed into a volume containing 460 engravings, whose superb hand-colouring replicates the iridescent hues of the originals. The title of the work, *Poissons, Ecrevisses, et Crabes, de Diverses Couleurs et Figures Extraordinaires, que l'on Trouve Autour des Isles Moloques, et sur les Côtes des Terres Australes* (Amsterdam 1718), indicates that some of the creatures

58 Hendrik Claudius, *Yellow Cobra*, 1685, watercolour, from MS. journal of Simon van der Stel's expedition to Namaqualand, The Board of Trinity College Dublin

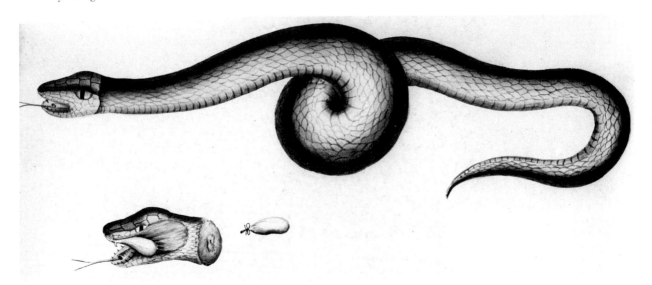

inhabited the waters of the Southland. Although to our eyes many of these appear to be complete inventions, a large number have been positively identified by marine biologists.[27] In his description of the 'Great Table Fish' (figure 59) the editor, Louis Renard, expresses the essence of this unique work:

> The curious of Holland, such as Messieurs Witsen, Scott, Scheynvoet, Vincent etc. have obtained several species of this sort of fish, however only the small varieties, some dried and others in bottles of wine spirits, but their most beautiful colors are lost ...

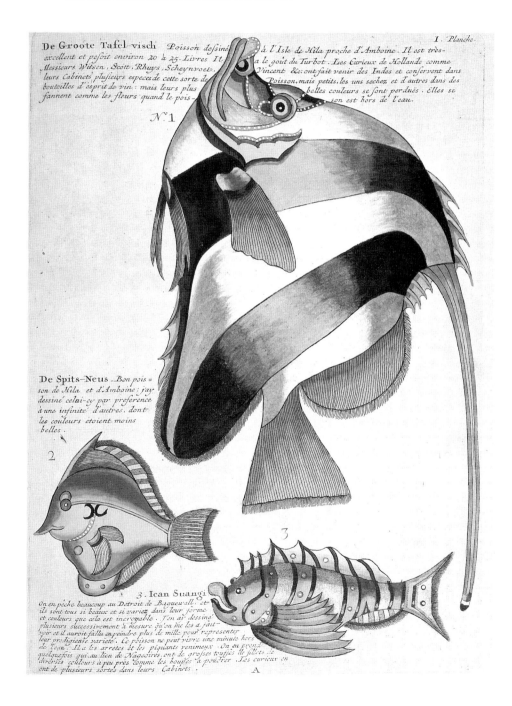

59 Louis Renard after Samuel Fallours, *The Great Table Fish*, 1718, hand-coloured engraving from *Poissons, Ecrevisses et Crabes* ... (reproduced in colour following page 108)

The nature of the experience of the unknown is transferable only when the correct colours are present: the intense, unmodulated colours of the Renaissance and baroque, so much stronger than those of later periods, are the same brilliant hues which radiate from the leaves of the *Rotz Atlas* or the *Atlas van der Hem*. For the early images of the southern world are distinct from their successors, not only in terms of the 'information' they convey, but also as products of a particular time, a special sensibility. If the studies of the post-baroque age are often more 'correct', they are also less intense, more inhibited. They remind us that the history of the search for new worlds in the southern hemisphere took place over a very long period of time, and the images which reflect and form visions of the unknown are products of distinct epochs, each with its particular taste and aesthetic. They remind us that the history we are attempting to trace is imbued with contrasts and discontinuities, and that comparisons are often difficult to make.

In his publications Louis Renard employed the extraordinary coloured drawings of Samuel Fallours to produce his own collection of 'rarities', works which in a certain sense replicated the experience of viewing a great private collection. As Dutch voyages of exploration to the Great Southland became less frequent, the private library and the *kunstkammer* (or curiosity cabinet) became the loci of discussion and study regarding this little-known region. Within the limited space of these *kunstkammern* plants and animals, minerals and fossils, archaeological and ethnographic specimens were assembled into encyclopedias of Creation. In the early years of the eighteenth century, Terra Australis began to occupy a tangible place amongst the exotic lands represented in these collections of marvels.

The Great Southland and the Republic of Letters: Nicolaas Witsen and his *Kunstkammer*

12

In the second half of the seventeenth century the image of the Southland in the Netherlands was to a great extent housed within the private collection of one man: Nicolaas Witsen (1641–1717), burgomaster of Amsterdam and a director of the Verenigde Oostindische Compagnie (VOC) (figure 60). Witsen had extensive international contacts, facilitating his entry into the so-called 'Republic of Letters', a global network of scholars and collectors. Through an active exchange of notes, hypotheses and documentation – including drawings and specimens – a more detailed picture of Creation was revealed to

PETRVS SCHENK AD VIVVM PINXIT & Sculpſit 1701.

correspondents in Europe, Africa, Asia, and America. Witsen's intense desire
to acquire information regarding the Southland stimulated Dutch exploration
at the end of the seventeenth century and the beginning of the eighteenth
century, notably the expedition of Willem de Vlamingh (1696–97). Witsen's
patronage of exploration in Australian waters provides an essential contextual
framework for the second, more famous, voyage of the English navigator
William Dampier to New Holland in 1699.

Witsen was well-situated to pursue his interest in Terra Australis.[1] His
father Cornelis, as noted previously, was a driving force behind the Tasman
expeditions of 1642–44. As a young man Nicolaas acquired a broad

knowledge of the world outside Europe. His studies with the eminent
scholar Jacob Golius at Leiden University stimulated a lifelong interest in
Oriental culture, language and literature. In 1665 he travelled to Moscow,
where his family had conducted business for over fifty years. The young heir
took advantage of this experience to establish contacts with Samoyeds,
Tartars, and Persians, and to record his observations and discussions
concerning the vast regions lying beyond the city. The information obtained
in the course of this visit would form the basis of his map of Tartary
(1687), a work of great significance in the history of cartography. In an
autobiographical sketch written in 1711 he notes further that he 'drew
everything with his own hand and among other things the cities of Moscow,
Novgorod, Pleskov and many principal buildings'. The drawings were later
engraved and incorporated into the *Atlas van der Hem*. They constitute
evidence of Nicolaas's interest in draughtsmanship (an interest shared by his
brother Jonas, who studied with the eminent painter Jan Lievens). For
Witsen, as for Banks and his contemporaries, the visual image would
constitute a vital tool of research.[2]

Upon his return from Russia Witsen travelled to Italy and France, and
soon afterwards to England, where he studied for a year at Oxford. In the
course of his studies and travels he acquired a systematic knowledge of ship
construction, delineated in his first publication, *Aeloude en hedendaegsche
scheeps-bouw en bestier* (Amsterdam 1671), a comprehensive investigation into
naval architecture and its history throughout the world. Witsen imparted his
knowledge of the field to Czar Peter the Great in the course of the latter's
voyages to the Netherlands, for which he served as official host. The Dutch
scholar's writings and collections pertaining to Asia benefited greatly, in turn,
from his friendship with the ruler of the vast Russian empire.

Shortly after the publication of his *Scheeps-bouw*, Witsen began a
career of public service which enhanced his status and intellectual contacts
internationally. In 1674 he was appointed burgomaster of Amsterdam, a
position he would hold on eight occasions. He played an important role in the
diplomatic process leading to the coronation of William of Orange as king of
England in 1689. As ambassador of the United Provinces during this period
he most assuredly renewed his contacts with British naturalists, including
Martin Lister, a leading specialist in conchology. His works were greatly
admired by Gottfried Wilhelm Leibniz, with whom he shared an interest in
Chinese culture and religion, revealed in letters exchanged over a period of
many years.[3]

As his extensive correspondence with the classicist Gisbert Cuper of
Deventer clearly demonstrates,[4] Witsen made full use of his position in the
Amsterdam hierarchy and the VOC to pursue his scholarly interests. As a
director of the VOC he had access to a vast quantity of reports pertaining to
Asia and Africa prepared by Company servants in Persia, South Africa, India,
Ceylon, southeast Asia, the East Indies, Formosa and Japan. He developed
good relationships with VOC governors interested in science; for example,
Simon van der Stel at the Cape of Good Hope[5] and Joan van Hoorn in

Batavia. Through his good offices one of his protégés, Herbert de Jager, a gifted Orientalist and botanical draughtsman, became head of the VOC office in Isfahan; the scientific research of Engelbert Kaempfer in Japan and the Near East also received his strong support.

The extensive resources of Witsen's family likewise contributed to the growth of his knowledge and collections. He acquired extensive material through contacts of his wife, Catherine de Hochepied, whom Witsen married in 1674. Her family was engaged in commercial undertakings in Russia; her relatives also served as Dutch representatives in Constantinople and Smyrna. Through his nephew Jonas Witsen, who possessed extensive holdings in the Dutch South American colony of Surinam, he obtained extensive accounts and specimens of the flora, fauna, and native peoples of tropical America.

61 After Maria Syballa Merian, *Moth, Caterpillar, Snake and other Creatures of Surinam*, 1705, engraving from M. S. Merian, *Metamorphosis Insectorum Surinamensium*

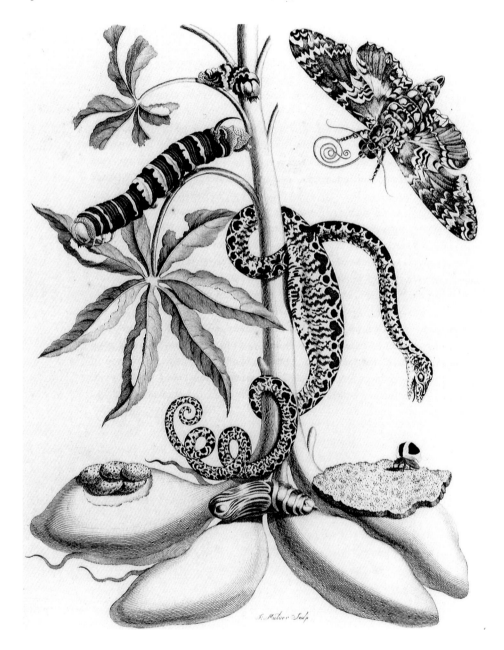

In the course of Witsen's investigations visual imagery was a crucial means of study, documentation, and divulgence of information. His employment of graphic media went beyond collecting and publishing illustrative material, however, and extended to the support of artists' travels in distant lands. In addition to the studies of Kaempfer and de Jager, Witsen took an interest in the work of Maria Syballa Merian, whose watercolours of insects, spiders, and serpents are imbued with a startling emotional intensity. He encouraged her efforts both in the Netherlands and in the course of her two-year sojourn in Surinam (1699–1701). The result of this American expedition was a masterful volume of plates, *Metamorphosis Insectorum Surinamensium* (Amsterdam 1705), a classic work of zoological illustration (figure 61).[6]

In the person of the indefatigable artist-traveller Cornelis de Bruijn, Witsen found the perfect instrument to further his investigations.[7] Although generally ignored in the modern art historical literature, de Bruijn was well-known in his lifetime as a result of his successful book, *Reizen over Moskovie, door Persie en Indië* (Amsterdam 1711), translated into English as *Travels into Muscovy, Persia and part of the East Indies* (London 1737). A superb portrait of the author by Sir Godfrey Kneller in the Rijksmuseum attests to his fame among his contemporaries (figure 62). De Bruijn's account of his Grand Tour is illustrated with his depictions of plants and animals, native people, archeological sites and views from many parts of Asia and the East Indies. His journeys were enthusiastically supported by Witsen, who incorporated the artist's paintings and drawings in his vast *kunstkammer* in Amsterdam. A significant part of the *Reizen* is devoted to the ruins of Persepolis; the plates after de Bruijn's designs would constitute the standard reproductions of the monument for over a century.[8] The great value Witsen placed upon de Bruijn's efforts is revealed in the Amsterdam patrician's correspondence with Gisbert Cuper. One letter (1 January 1713) is devoted to a painstaking critique of certain plates of Persepolis in Jean Chardin's *Voyages en Perse et aux Indes orientales* (1686); inaccuracies of detail in the French work were determined with the aid of de Bruijn's precise notes and renderings.[9]

The material accumulated by Witsen through his collecting and patronage was catalogued and arranged in his museum of curiosities in Amsterdam. The auction catalogue of this collection published in 1728, eleven years after its owner's death, provides an overview of its contents.[10] These include items from all parts of the world: gold jewelry from Tartar tombs in Siberia, a vast collection of Chinese, Mogul, and Japanese miniatures, plates of animals, plants, birds and insects, Asian weaponry, fossil remains of prehistoric animals, a series of paintings of exotic subjects including twenty-four portraits of the Turkish aristocracy by Cornelis de Bruijn, and antique fragments (including a bas-relief from Persepolis removed from the monument by de Bruijn). One cabinet held a Blaeu atlas of nine volumes, supplemented by numerous maps, charts, and views of Asia, the East Indies, Australia, New Guinea, and Russia. The natural history collections were very extensive as well. A cabinet made of wood from Ambon

62 Godfrey Kneller,
Cornelis de Bruijn, ca.
1700, oil on canvas,
Rijksmuseum–Stichting,
Amsterdam (reproduced in
colour following page 108)

held forty-five drawers filled with shells, corals, minerals, plants and animals.
Lining the walls, there were 245 animal specimens preserved in flasks
of alcohol, and a cedarwood cabinet of eighteen drawers held a special
collection of insects and spiders from Surinam, possibly related to the work
of Maria Syballa Merian.

Witsen's museum was undoubtedly complemented by a vast library,
whose contents are not included in the auction record. These extremely
varied materials were employed in the pursuit of their owner's research into
the physical features of the world, the possible relationships linking diverse
cultures and languages, and the origins of skin colour. Witsen wished to
reconcile all of this data with his firm Christian belief in the unity of God's
creation. Specimens acquired in all parts of the world attested to the infinite

variety of living things produced by Divine Will. The cultural evidence he acquired was employed as a means of demonstrating the derivation of all religious systems from Judaism and early Christianity. Witsen's traditional Christian views are articulated in nearly every letter to Gisbert Cuper, corroborated by references to works in his collection and library.

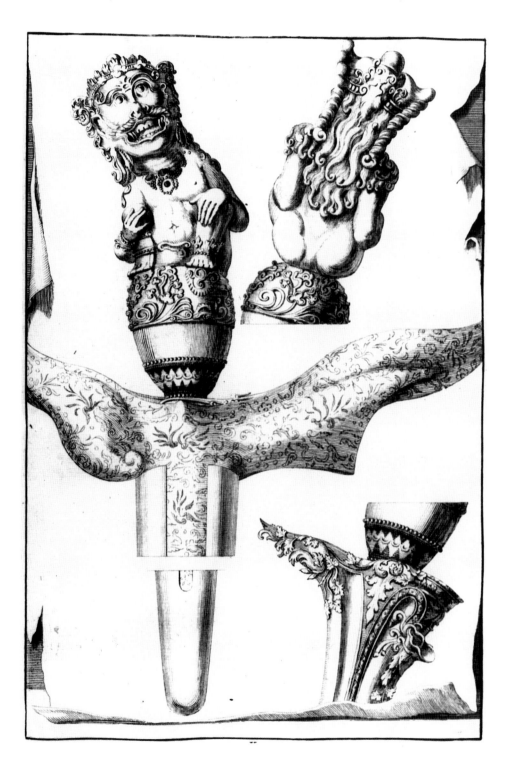

63 Javanese Kris from the Collection of Nicolaas Witsen, 1705, engraving from Nicolaas Witsen, *Noord en Oost Tartarye*, Mitchell Library, State Library of New South Wales

Nevertheless, as Rietbergen has correctly noted,[11] Witsen was far more critical of the reports of strange phenomena than his correspondent, far more willing to investigate the non-Western, non-Christian world. In this respect he may be said to represent a transitional figure between the classical era and the Enlightenment.

The principal focus of Witsen's attention was a region which he designated as 'north and east Tartary', an area bounded on the west by Muscovy, on the east by the Pacific Ocean, and on the south by the Himalayas.[12] The cultures of Terra Australis, the Pacific islands, and the Americas were viewed as extensions of this region; the venerable Chinese civilization lay at its centre. Like many scholars of his generation Witsen was fascinated by Chinese culture and learning. In the works of Confucius, whom he compared with Seneca and Plato, he detected traces of a primitive monotheism. With his correspondent Leibniz he shared a desire for the establishment of a Protestant mission to parallel the Jesuit undertaking in China. However, Witsen was less idealistic, less utopian in his vision. As a strict Calvinist he did not seek the reciprocal spiritual enlightenment between East and West so fervently desired by Leibniz. Nevertheless, the German philosopher was drawn to the Dutch amateur as a man with a great deal of information as well as unique contacts and resources to facilitate scholarly efforts.[13]

The fruits of Witsen's investigations and – to a limited extent – the contents of his collection can be studied in his major work, *Noord en Oost Tartarye* (first edition, Amsterdam 1692; second edition, Amsterdam 1705). In the splendid plates illustrating the text we receive a view into his *kunstkammer*: superb objects of Scythian gold, finely wrought Javanese daggers or krises (figure 63), fossil remains of mammoths unearthed in Siberia – all presented in brilliantly executed engravings. In the second edition Witsen reproduced for the first time the illustrations in Tasman's journal, together with the most extensive account of the expedition that had yet been published.

The Expedition of

Willem de Vlamingh

to the Great Southland (1696–97)

Although the VOC's interest in the Southland waned during the course of the second half of the seventeenth century, the fascination which the region held for geographers and amateurs remained constant. This was certainly the case

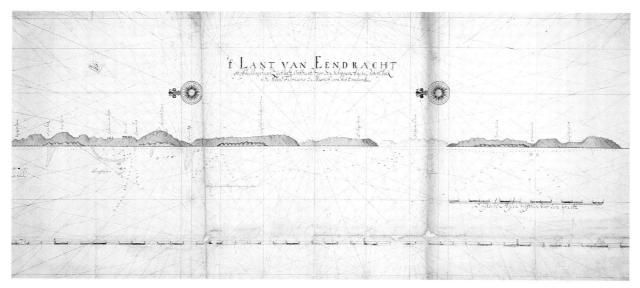

64 Johan Nessel, *View of Australia's West Coast*, 1658, watercolour, pen and pencil, Algemeen Rijksarchief, The Hague (reproduced in colour following page 140)

for Nicolaas Witsen, perhaps the sole member of the Republic of Letters with the means of satisfying his curiosity concerning the ill-defined Terra Australis.

Accordingly, Witsen followed the reports of accidental sightings of the southern continent with great interest. In 1656 the VOC ship *De Gulden Draeck* ran aground and sank on the west coast of Australia at latitude 30° 40" South. Seven survivors reached Batavia in a small vessel with the news that 118 men had died but sixty-eight remained alive on the coast. A rescue expedition was launched under the command of Samuel Volckertsz and Aucke Pieters Jonck to find the supposed survivors and explore the coast.[14] Although the Dutch ships found no trace of the ship or its crew, their voyage did result in the drafting of a superb coastal profile by Johan Nessel nearly 1.2 metres long (figure 64).[15] In the midst of the massive cliffs looming up from the sea is a plain (on the left of the figure) wherein three schematically rendered Aboriginal huts are depicted. In addition to this imposing image, another tangible result of the voyage of Volckertsz and Jonck was the recovery of an Aboriginal hammer or kodj found on the shore.[16] The object, the first Aboriginal artefact known to have existed in a European collection, was carefully examined and described some years afterwards by Witsen in Amsterdam.[17]

The wreck of *De Gulden Draeck* and its aftermath must have served to increase Witsen's curiosity. In the auction catalogue of his collection there is a reference to two maps of the northeast portion of the Southland, executed in the course of the voyage of Jan van der Waal in *De Vliegende Swaan* (1678).[18] When the opportunity to organize a new expedition presented itself, as it did in the mid-1690s, he was well prepared.

In 1695 the VOC planned another in a series of periodic missions to find one of its ships lost at sea. In this instance the missing vessel was the *Ridderschap van Holland*, which had vanished east of the Cape of Good Hope.

Witsen took an active role in the preparation of this rescue expedition, transforming it into a scientific voyage to examine the lands, natural history, resources, and native people of New Holland's west coast.[19] Three vessels were outfitted: the *Geelvinck*, the *Nijptangh*, and the *t'Weseltje*. Command of the ships and 198 men was given to Willem de Vlamingh. Witsen insisted upon the presence of two artists on the voyage to render all coastlines and inland waters, as well as the rarities to be found in the Southland.[20] One of the artists selected was Victor Victorszoon, son of the well-known painter Jan Victors. It was hoped that the expedition would also capture a native who might be trained as an interpreter to obtain further information.[21]

On 30 December 1696 the expedition reached New Holland at 31° South. In the course of the following two months the ships sailed southward to latitude 20° South, finding no trace of the *Ridderschap van Holland*. De Vlamingh explored a number of sites in present-day Western Australia: the Swan River, Island Point and Gantheaume Bay. No Aborigines were sighted, but evidence of their presence was duly noted: huts two to three feet high built of poles with branches and leaves placed against them and a bag made out of animal skin. De Vlamingh brought the bag with him for Witsen's inspection, together with a number of specimens.

In spite of its careful planning, the de Vlamingh expedition was a disappointment to its patron. The only material items received by Witsen were some branches of wood and 'a small chest containing shells collected on the beaches, fruits, plants etc.'. Depictions of two of the shells would accompany a letter by Witsen to Martin Lister, published in the *Philosophical Transactions* of the Royal Society in 1698. According to de Vlamingh's report, a number of drawings of aquatic animals were apparently executed, although neither these pictures nor the images of the shells have been located. Several black swans were captured but died during the course of the return voyage. No specimens of land animals were obtained; however, Witsen records de Vlamingh's discovery of marsupial quokkas, described as:

> a large number of bush rats, nearly as big as cats, which had a pouch
> below their throats into which one could put one's hand, without being
> able to understand to what end nature had created the animal like this:
> as soon as it had been shot dead, this animal smelled terribly, so that
> the skins were not taken along.[22]

The most extraordinary documentation of the voyage is a series of eighteen watercolour views by Victor Victorszoon, fifteen of which depict the west coast of Australia (figure 65).[23] These sensitive, atmospheric landscapes would have undoubtedly pleased their patron, but they apparently were never delivered; Witsen complained bitterly about their disappearance. Presumed lost for nearly three centuries, they were discovered by Günter Schilder in 1970 in the Maritiem Museum 'Prins Hendrik', Rotterdam. Victorszoon's renderings – the earliest comprehensive views of the western Australian shoreline – are executed with an extraordinary delicacy and economy of line.

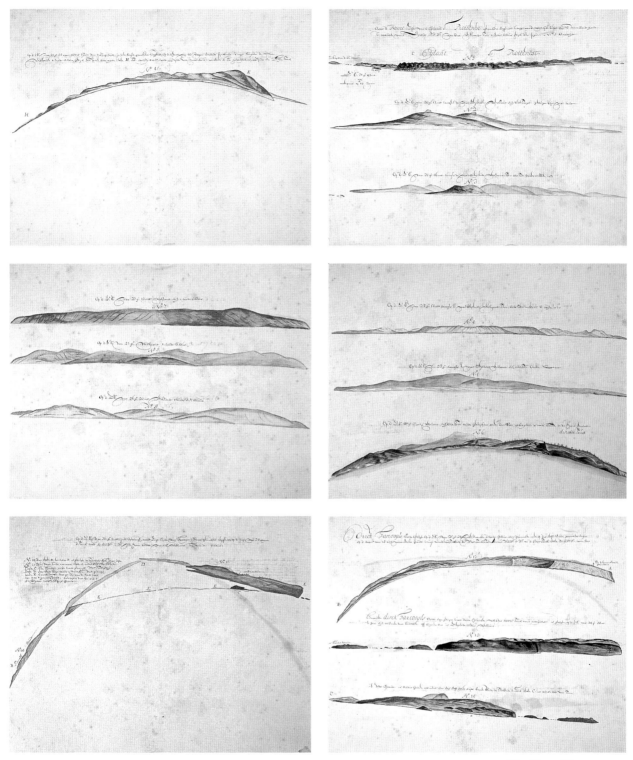

They compare favourably in quality with the evocative views of the misty coasts of Madeira executed by Frans Post for Johan Maurits a half-century earlier.[24]

The disappearance of Victorszoon's paintings constituted only one of the expedition's failings in the eyes of its patron. The ships departed for

65 Victor Victorszoon, *Coastal Views of Western Australia*, 1696-97, watercolours, Maritiem Museum 'Prins Hendrik', Rotterdam (reproduced in colour following page 140)

Batavia from North West Cape on 21 February 1697 without having fulfilled Witsen's expectations. Of the two artists engaged on the voyage, Victorszoon was the only one who actually sailed to New Holland. No Southlander was brought back to the Netherlands, nor was any thorough investigation of the western part of New Holland undertaken. In a letter to Cuper Witsen ascribes the failure of the venture to the drunkenness of its leader, who never remained in any locality for more than three days.[25] Witsen's complaints appear to echo van Diemen's derogatory remarks concerning Tasman. In the

66 Victor Victorszoon after Willem de Vlamingh, *The Southland*, 1697, MS. on paper, Algemeen Rijksarchief, The Hague

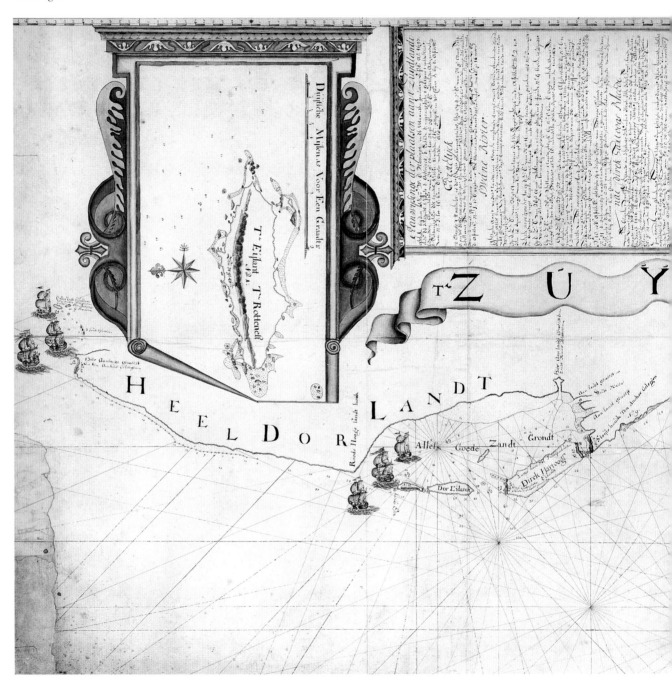

seventeenth century, the available means for conducting a careful study in Australian waters were not adequate to satisfy inquisitive minds.

The principal visual record of de Vlamingh's voyage accessible to his contemporaries is a manuscript chart of western Australia by Victor Victorszoon, a beautifully detailed work more than 1.5 metres in length (figure 66).[26] In general, the Dutch public remained unaware of the results of the expedition, and it was not until 1753 that a full description, illustrated with a comprehensive map of de Vlamingh's discoveries, was published in the Netherlands.[27]

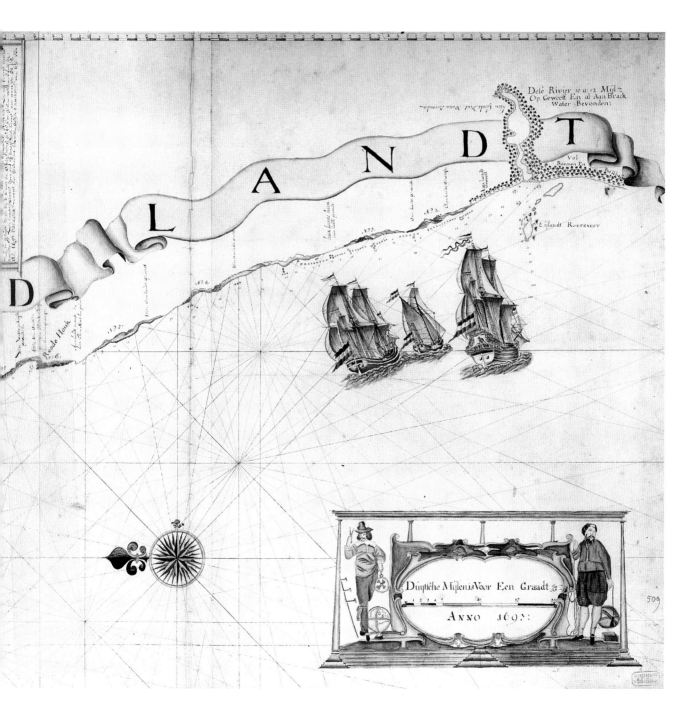

William Dampier in

New Holland and New Britain

(1699–1700)

One year after Witsen's letter summarizing the results of de Vlamingh's voyage was published in the Royal Society's *Philosophical Transactions*, William Dampier cast anchor in the same location on the west coast of New Holland visited by the Dutch explorer (now called Shark Bay in accordance with the name employed by the British navigator).[28] Although historians have not linked the two voyages, it is significant that Dampier had established important contacts among British scholars who were colleagues of Nicolaas Witsen in the international Republic of Letters.

Eleven years earlier Dampier had arrived on the northern shores of New Holland in the buccaneer vessel the *Cygnet*. His description of the Aborigines encountered on that occasion, as published in his *New Voyage round the World* (1697), has often been quoted as a prime example of the European's inability to comprehend the native inhabitants of Australia:

> The Inhabitants of this Country are the miserablest People in the World ... setting aside their Humane Shape, they differ but little from Brutes. They are tall, strait-bodied, and thin, with small long Limbs. They have great Heads, round Foreheads, and great Brows. Their Eyelids are always half closed, to keep the Flies out of their Eyes ... They are long-visaged, and of a very unpleasing Aspect, having no one graceful Feature in their Faces. Their Hair is black, short and curl'd, like that of the Negroes; and not long and lank like the Common Indians: The Colour of their Skins, both of their Faces and the rest of their Body, is Coal-black, like that of the Negroes of Guinea.[29]

Dampier's description, which appeared in the numerous editions of this extremely popular work, does not do justice to his abilities as an observer. As Glyndwr Williams has noted, the manuscript version of the text contains a more dispassionate account; the description of the Aborigines' hair, in particular, corresponds more precisely with reality:

> They are a people of good stature but very thin and leane I judge for want of food [;] they are black yett I belive their haires would be long, if it was combed out but for want of Combs it is matted up like a negroes haire.[30]

Perhaps the longer, more sensational description may have seemed more appealing to Dampier or his publisher, more interested in selling copies than in ethnological truth. In any event, the explorer's second voyage would provide significant, if limited, information about the Southland to the British scholarly community.

The publication of the *New Voyage* in 1697 appears to have drawn the attention of the British government to Dampier's knowledge of the waters of the South Seas. One may suppose that the publication of Witsen's letter to Lister the following year may also have encouraged British attempts to launch their own investigation of the Southland. However, like the Dutch, the British were reluctant to initiate any major voyages of exploration, preferring to concentrate upon coasts and seas which were known to be commercially profitable.[31] Their limited contribution to Dampier's venture reflected their conservative attitude: a leaky vessel with a crew of fifty men instead of the seventy he had requested.

Dampier arrived in New Holland in August 1699 aboard the rather unseaworthy *Roebuck*. Sailing to the northeast, his encounters with the natives were short and violent, his impressions of the land were negative. He did, however, collect a number of plant specimens – the earliest extant records of Australian flora. Abandoning the barren coast of New Holland, he travelled along the northern coast of New Guinea, hoping to discover new sources of spices or other natural products. The island of New Britain, situated to the east of the land of the Papuans – and lying near the region discovered by Tasman fifty-seven years earlier sailing in the opposite direction – appeared to fulfil this goal. Dampier observed that 'this Island may afford as many rich Commodities as any in the World'.[32]

Dampier's expedition did not add very much to knowledge of the Southland already gathered from Dutch voyages. However, despite the loss of the *Roebuck* on the return voyage in 1700, together with many of his papers, Dampier managed to bring back precious evidence of natural forms and human cultures. A small collection of dried plants and native artefacts was presented to Dr John Woodward, a Fellow of the Royal Society and a prominent figure in the early history of what would become known as paleontology. Dampier's specimens of Australian plants were in turn donated by Woodward to his friend William Sherard (founder of the Sherardian Chair of Botany at Oxford) in 1710, together with his entire botanical collection. Woodward, however, retained the two stone artefacts acquired by Dampier in New Britain within his superb collection of fossils, still preserved in its original case in the Sedgwick Museum of Geology, Cambridge.[33]

Among the specimens from New Holland in the Sherardian Herbarium, one of the finest is the '*Clianthus formosus*', or 'Sturt's desert pea' (figure 67). The appearance of this attractive plant is recorded in the engraving published in Dampier's *A Voyage to New Holland etc. in the Year 1699* (London 1703) (figure 68). The plate was clearly executed by an artist with more skill than the draughtsman responsible for the very crude images of bird and marine life in the same volume (perhaps Dampier himself).[34] The two stone artefacts from New Britain, an axe head (figure 69) and a slingstone,[35] 'may be the earliest "authenticated" objects from the region', predating by seventy years the Aboriginal spears collected by Cook in Botany Bay.[36]

67 *Sturt's desert pea*, specimen collected in Western Australia by William Dampier in 1699, Sherardian Herbarium, Department of Plant Sciences, University of Oxford

The characteristic 'waisted' form of the axe head most certainly appealed to Dampier, whose preference for the strange objects encountered in New Britain is demonstrated in a passage from *A Voyage to New Holland*:

They [the islanders] are very dextrous, active Fellows in their Proes, which are very ingeniously built. They are narrow and long, with Out-

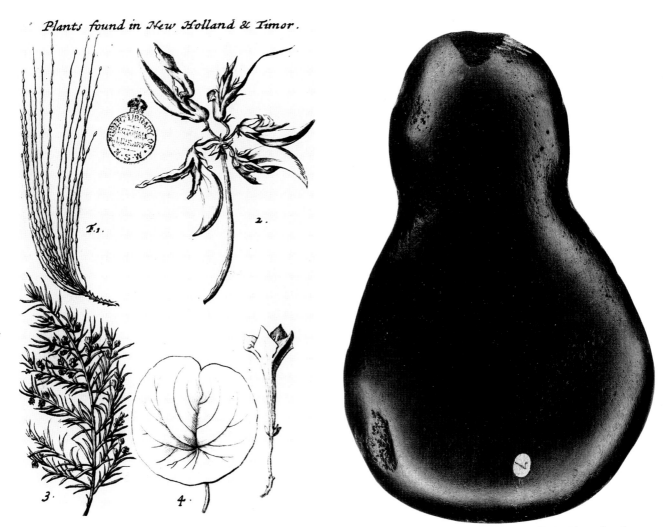

Plants found in New Holland & Timor.

lagers on one side; the Head and Stern higher than the rest, and carved into many Devices, viz. some Fowl, Fish or a Man's Head, painted or carv'd: And although it's but rudely done, yet the Resemblance appears plainly, and shews an ingenious Fancy. But with what Instruments they make their Proes or carved work, I know not; for they seem to be utterly ignorant of Iron.[37]

68 **(left)** Plants found in New Holland and Timor, 1703, engraving from William Dampier, *A Voyage to New Holland, etc., in the Year 1699*, Mitchell Library, State Library of New South Wales

69 **(right)** Stone axe head, New Britain, before 1700, Sedgwick Museum of Geology, Cambridge

With the publication of Dampier's *A Voyage to New Holland* in 1703, and reproductions of Isaac Gilsemans's illustrations of Tabar Island canoes in Witsen's *Noord en Oost Tartarye* two years later, Melanesian art was incorporated into the European repertory of forms for the first time. The comments made by Haalbos and Dampier suggest that the reaction to these carvings on the part of navigators – and, presumably, collectors such as Witsen – was one of fascination and delight.

It is intriguing to speculate as to the possibility of exchanges between Nicolaas Witsen and Dampier's circle concerning the Southland. Whether Dampier himself was aware of Witsen's publications is perhaps questionable, as no English translation of Witsen's works exists. Certainly, Witsen would have been capable of reading the accounts of Dampier's voyages, which undoubtedly would have interested him. He was also aware of the collections and studies of John Woodward; in a letter to Cuper of 9 April 1713 he warmly recommends the writings of the English scholar.[38] Further research into the correspondence of the leading British naturalists of the period may well shed light upon this question.

Whether or not the Dutch had any interest in Dampier's plant specimens, artefacts, or his comments regarding Melanesian carvings, it is certain that they did not look favourably upon his incursions into their territory. Accordingly, they outfitted expeditions to conduct their own investigations in northern Australia and New Guinea, as a means of circumventing any potential threat to their trade monopoly in the East Indies. In 1705 three ships under the command of Maarten van Delft sailed to the northeast corner of Arnhem Land. The brief report of this voyage did not alter the negative image of the Aborigine, described as stark naked, very poor, primitive and evil-natured.[39]

Of greater significance in terms of the subject of Terra Australis was the expedition of Jacob Weyland to New Guinea aboard the *Geelvinck* in the same year; as this voyage never reached New Holland it has been ignored in the chronicles of the discovery of Australia.[40] Arriving on the northern coast of the island, Weyland explored and charted the bay which would bear the name of his vessel (now Tjenderawasih Bay, Irian Jaya); a manuscript map by Isaac de Graff in the Algemeen Rijksarchief records the results of the voyage.[41] Four Papuans seized by Weyland in Jobi and in the village of Kui in the vicinity of Geelvinck Bay were brought back to Batavia. Their presence in the capital of the Dutch East Indies was noted with great interest by Cornelis de Bruijn, who was visiting Java at the same moment. In his *Reizen over Moskovie, door Persie en Indië*, de Bruijn informs us that the captives ' ... were treated in this manner, that they might have an opportunity of representing the humanity of the Company to their fellow natives, and to induce them to engage in commerce with our nation ...'.[42] The painter's eye was caught by these exceptional 'curiosities' collected like rare butterflies in the little-known regions to the south: 'These savages had something so peculiar in their air, that I had an inclination to paint one with his bow and arrow in his hand, agreeably to their manner, and as may be seen in plate 197'.[43] In the engraving executed after de Bruijn's drawing (figure 70) the impassive, muscular figure draws back on his bow while clutching several arrows in his left hand. Presumably prepared under the artist's supervision, the figure and his weaponry are rendered with the same care taken over the images of the ruins of Persepolis reproduced elsewhere in the same volume.

Whereas de Bruijn suggests that the decision to depict the Southlander and his weapons was his own, he must have thought that the subject would have a special importance for his client, Witsen, in Amsterdam. Of the four captives, three were transported to the Netherlands.[44] We know that two of them met and spoke with Nicolaas Witsen, who did not miss the opportunity to commission their portraits.[45] Seventy years before the exuberant reception

70 After
Cornelis de Bruijn,
A Southlander,
1711, engraving
from C. de Bruijn,
*Reizen over
Moskovie, door
Persie en Indië*,
Mitchell Library,
State Library of
New South Wales

of the Tahitian Omai in British aristocratic circles, these Papuans, representatives of what was considered to be a far less attractive 'race', were on view before the patrician elite in the great international marketplace of Amsterdam.

The circumstances of the interview are described in a letter written by Gijsbert Cuper to another collector, Pieter Valckenier in 1709. The two Southlanders, who had learned Malay, were questioned on Witsen's behalf by sailors. Frightened by the prospect of enslavement upon their return to Batavia, they sought refuge in the Netherlands. Whereas one of the men had succeeded in obtaining employment as a carpenter in the shipyards, the other had failed to learn any trade. When questioned as to whether they were married, one of them began to weep, apparently moved by the memory of his wife and family.[46] The pathos of this scene is in marked contrast with the relatively idealized image of the Papuan warrior transmitted by de Bruijn.

The native of Geelvinck Bay was not the only 'specimen' from the Southland to be studied and drawn by Cornelis de Bruijn, as he informs us in another passage from the *Reizen*:

> While I was at our general's [Joan van Hoorn] I saw a certain animal called a Filander, which has something very extraordinary in it ... It has a head like fox, and a pointed tail; but what is most extraordinary in it is, that it has a bag under its belly, into which the young ones retreat even when they are very large ...[47]

De Bruijn's image of this creature (figure 71) is the earliest-known portrayal of a wallaby which, we may assume, was collected either in New Guinea by Weyland or in Australia by van Delft. Once again, we may be certain that the significance of the engraving would have been thoroughly understood by Witsen. Two 'filanders' corresponding to de Bruijn's description – one with its young – were preserved in alcohol in Witsen's collection.[48] A close relative of the animal which would become the most renowned symbol of modern Australia had already been studied, drawn and collected long before Cook's first voyage. It is indeed possible that the Dutch were not the first to encounter wallabies or kangaroos; the pouched animal depicted on the title-page of Gerard and Cornelis de Jode's *Speculum Orbis Terrae* (1597)[49] may have been inspired by an early Spanish voyage to New Guinea.

The collections and commissions of Nicolaas Witsen are especially important for reconstructing the image of the Southland in the Netherlands circa 1700. While obviously the subject was of special interest to the Amsterdam burgomaster, other members of his elite group shared his curiosity. Within their own cabinets they incorporated whatever specimens they could obtain from the region. François Valentijn in his *Oud en Nieuw Oost-Indiën* indicates where one could view rare and beautiful shells from the waters of Terra Australis in the Netherlands. In addition to Valentijn's, there were the collections of Simon Schynvoet in Amsterdam, of Francis Kiggelaar in The Hague, Antony van Dishoek in Vlissingen, and of the still-life painter Karel Borchaert Voet.[50]

71 After Cornelis de Bruijn, *A Wallaby*, 1711, engraving from C. de Bruijn, *Reizen over Moskovie, door Persie en Indië*, Mitchell Library, State Library of New South Wales

The shells in Dutch cabinets, together with the other visual documents we have examined, contributed to the formulation of certain impressions of the Southland, its flora, fauna, and human inhabitants in the early eighteenth century. The space devoted to it within the museums of the world would expand significantly at the end of the century as a result of the voyages of Cook and his successors; nevertheless, the Southland had already secured a place within the western consciousness.

The Southland in the Writings

of Nicolaas Witsen

Seated amidst his many books and objects, Witsen tried to make sense of what he had read and collected regarding the Southland over the years. In his *Noord en Oost Tartarye* he incorporated its inhabitants within his own vision of the origins and movements of the world's population since Creation. His writings provide valuable insights into the image of the southern world and its people in early eighteenth century Holland. In the course of his discussion Witsen directly confronts one of the most difficult problems facing his contemporaries: how had the Southland, the Pacific, and South America been populated? As an expert on cartography, ethnography, and shipbuilding, the Amsterdam patrician believed that he had the correct answers.

Witsen was convinced that many of the peoples of this extensive southern region migrated from Tartary, China, Japan, and 'Yeso' (a land thought to stretch from the eastern Kuril Islands to the American mainland).[51] A careful examination of the cartographic documents (for example, Nicolas Sanson's world map of 1678, see figure 43) would reveal that Formosa, the Philippines, the Moluccas, and the chains of Pacific islands were easily accessible from the Asian mainland by means of the canoes customarily employed by these people. In no more than three days it would be possible to sail to New Guinea, New Holland, and then to the Statenland (New Zealand, still thought to be linked to the lands lying near Tierra del Fuego). Without any knowledge of sailing upon the open seas, therefore, almost the entire region could be reached from the Asian population centres. Only the more remote areas, such as the Marianas, were inaccessible by canoe. These however would have been settled by the South Sea islanders, 'who are good sailors, and who use sailing boats, which can sail close to the wind'.[52]

If the study of maps enables us to comprehend how the more remote regions of the world were settled, a knowledge of history, geography, and ethnography reveals why this massive migration took place. Witsen argues that it is generally known that the islands lying closest to the mainland of north Asia are the most densely populated, and that New Guinea – the entranceway into Terra Australis – has more inhabitants than the regions lying further south. This process of population displacement is said to parallel developments in the East Indies. Prior to the arrival of Christians, the populations of Ternate, Banda, Ambon, and other islands were much larger than populations of the areas lying further to the south and west. Upon the arrival of more civilized people, the original uncivilized inhabitants were compelled to migrate to Ceram, New Guinea, and even more remote lands. The dislocation of savage peoples from more densely populated areas, generally lying to the north, to more remote, usually more southerly regions is developed into a universal principle, applied to the movements of people from the Philippines into the South Pacific as well as the migration of American native populations from north to south.

Evidence of skin colour constituted another means of determining the diverse Asian origins of the peoples of the Southland. Employing this standard of evaluation, however, Witsen falls into a contradiction. The brown flesh tones of the New Zealanders appeared to link them with their supposed American brethren, leading him to advance the theory:

> that these people in this country [New Zealand] have also come from
> America or the Tierra del Fuego; it has also been said, that they or

64 Johan Nessel, *View of Australia's West Coast*, 1658, watercolour, pen and pencil, Algemeen Rijksarchief, The Hague

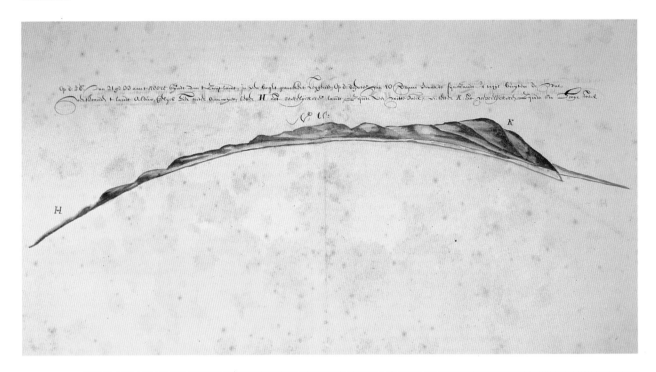

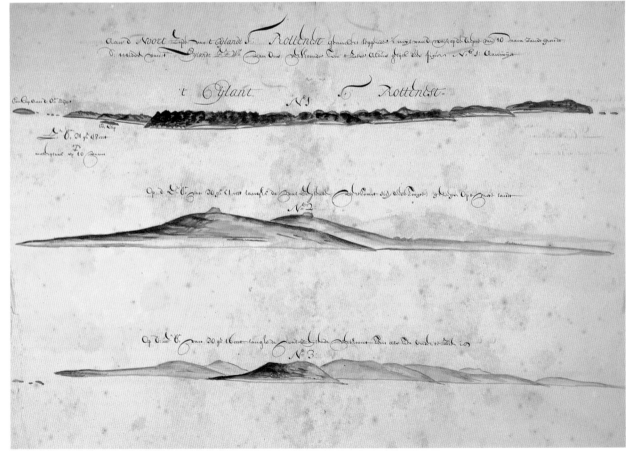

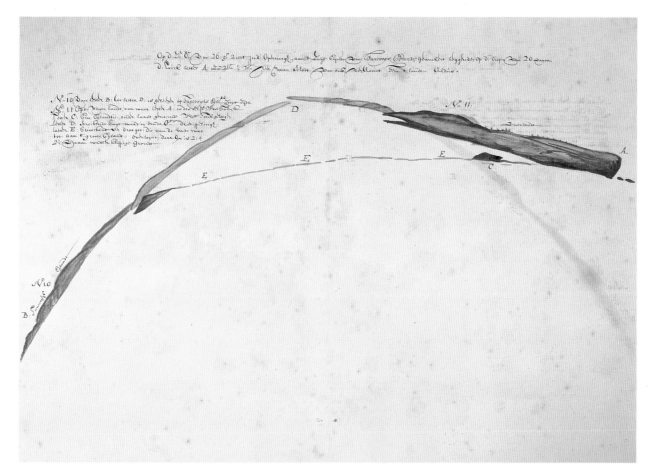

Op d' Z:O van 26 g: Ziet md Ophringh aan t' suyt Eynde van Tartoogs Eylandt: ghanckbr Vgghdis: op d' Diepte zyn 20 vaam
d' Noort wnt A: zzW:t:W: Het binnen Mor van ons ghMorwt: Voor t' land Aldus:

N:o 10 Dan dirck B: bet letter D: is ghelegn op Tartoogs Oost Zuyt dye
N:o 11 Op t' vaam land van voor dirck A: in dir O: West...
dirck C: Een Clipschi ond laech grome Eort sch...
dirck D: Spitschg Lage md in dirck O: dis Clipchig:
dirck E: Strechend sch droogi di van de baer vaa...
tot aan t' grosse Eylandt: ord lopen dire D: is 2:4
2½ vaam waetr Cippigr Grondr

N:o 11

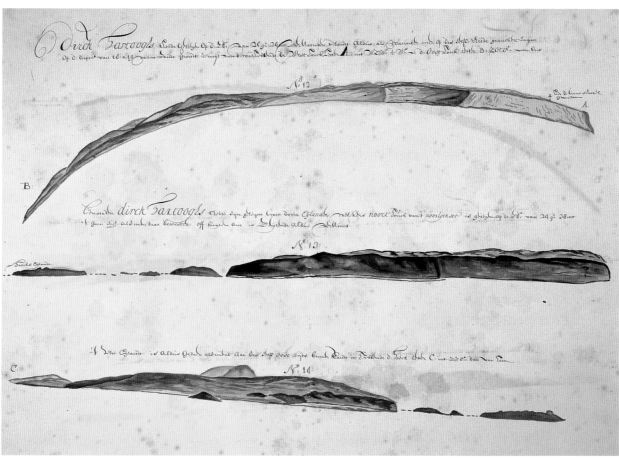

Dirck Tartoogs Lede ghelgh op d' Z:O van 26 g: 20 uur t' Noorden t' hany: Aldus als ghaanrke md op dis diep Reede ghanckbr lagen
Op d' Diepte van 18 al 19 vaam zaam Grondt t' nyt zand t Reed... de West Zouck dirck A int NZW: t:W: d' Voor Zouck dirk B: ZO:O: van Ons

N:o 12

Tussen dirck Tartoogs rolten syn ghelgn Enee Borre Eylandm: rolt dirs noort Zouck vant noordlyckst is ghelgh op di Z:O van 20 g: 30 uur
t' gen zig aldus md daar benost: off bynstn Ons W: Gghdaar aldus ghMorw:

N:o 13

Derck Eylandt

t' deze Eylandt is Aldis Gedaan aldindt Aan dir dieß Oost zyde binnd Naan in drökhdi d' dirk dirk C: int ZZ:O: dan van Een

N:o 14

C:

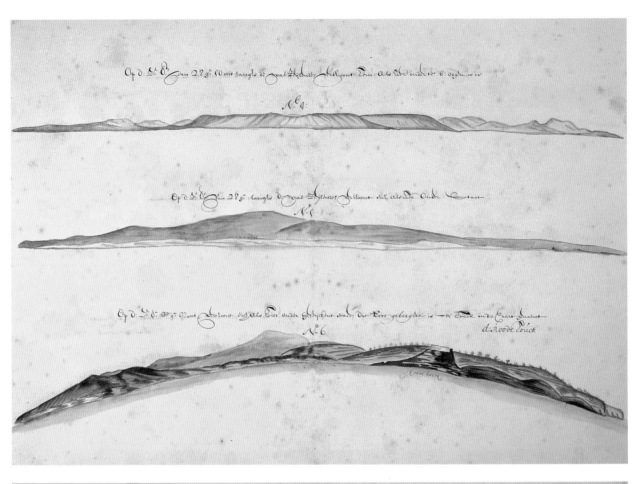

Op d: Z: W: van 28 g: 30 mt: langhs de wat Tafelbaÿ Brilpont Loin als t'W: onder N: 6: oogh: is is

N:e 4

Op d: Z: W: van 28 g: langhs de wat Tafelbaÿ Brilpont sich als een onder Straat

N:e 5

Op d: Z: W: 27 g: Waar Afelberch sich als Een oude gebÿckt: wat: Der Roor geberghen is—de Einde in de Eaart draÿat— d: Roode Clock

N: 6

Roode hoeck

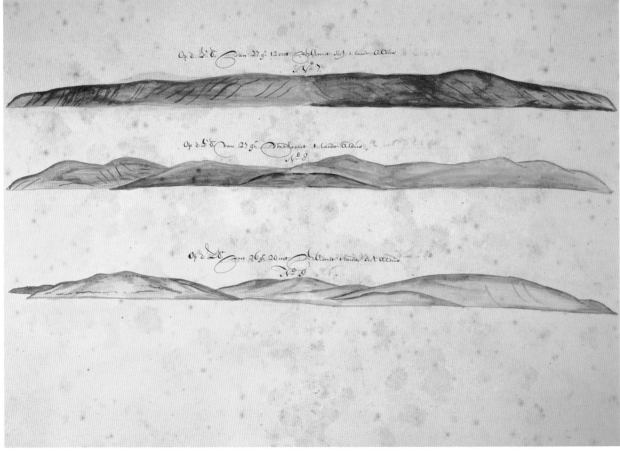

Op d: Z: W: van 27 g: 12 mt: Tafelboar sich t'laant aldus

N:e 7

Op d: Z: W: van 27 g: Afel-poent t'laant aldus

N: 8

Op d: Z: W: van 26 g: 30 mt: Afelbar t'laant dut aldus

N: 9

some of them perhaps originally came from the Indies islands, Japan, Yeso or Tartary across New Guinea, because the color of their skin and hair is most similar to the Americans, and that this land [New Zealand] stretches to Magellanica. The people of New Zealand, America, and Tartary belong to the same group, and those of New Holland, Papua New Guinea, the Moluccas and the Indian coast are derived from the middle of Asia.[53]

Elsewhere in his text, however, Witsen effectively negates this argument, employing traditional notions of the transmutation of skin tone. The blacks in the Southland, he observes, were originally light-skinned, north Asian people whose colour in the course of several generations became progressively darker as a result of exposure to the hot sun.[54] It is not surprising that Witsen's arguments are sometimes contradictory. Faced with such vexing problems as the origins of the races, and armed with so little concrete evidence, he resorted to the common beliefs of his age.

The principal leitmotif in Witsen's account of Terra Australis is the savagery of its people – at least that of the inhabitants of New Zealand, New Guinea, and New Holland. The South Sea islanders by contrast had acquired a certain technological superiority as demonstrated by their superior boats and seamanship. The Maoris, however, were people of a savage expression ('een wreede gezicht').[55] The Papuans and Aborigines were even worse, 'with a certain flash of redness sparkling through the blackness of their eyes, from which one can readily detect their bloodthirsty and murderous nature'.[56] Their malicious character could be readily demonstrated by the terrible fate of the young Dutch sailors who fell into their hands – slain, dragged into the woods, and eaten.

Witsen was intensely curious about the Southland – its topography, flora and fauna, as well as its inhabitants – a fascination which went well beyond any desire for commercially useful information on the part of a Company servant. Nevertheless, there can be no question as to the position of the Southland's 'hard' primitives within his global vision of humanity. In his imagination he visualized them as irredeemably degenerate savages, driven from their ancestral homes in Asia, pursued across New Guinea to the south. Witsen's firm belief in the hierarchy of human cultures based upon their level of 'civility' is evident in his writings and correspondence.

In his approach to specific subjects Witsen often appears surprisingly 'modern'. His careful description of the Aboriginal kodj recovered in 1658 – probably the earliest account of an Australian artefact ever written – is a model of objectivity and precision.[57] He correctly noted for example that the resin employed to attach the wooden handle to the stone head had been manufactured from the type of eucalyptus gum presented to him by Willem de Vlamingh. In Witsen's opinion, however, the most plausible use for this strange instrument was that of a deadly weapon, probably employed by Aboriginal cannibals against the unfortunate Dutch sailors stranded upon the beaches of western Australia. For Witsen the Aborigines were the inverse of the Chinese – the lowest level of humanity.

Terra Australis in the
Early Eighteenth Century

The bitter experiences of the Dutch and English in New Guinea, Australia, and New Zealand in the seventeenth and early eighteenth centuries did not destroy the shining image of Terra Australis. Faced with such discouraging reports Europeans turned their attention to the more promising lands to the east of New Holland. For these geographers, merchants, and would-be explorers, the glorious vision of Terra Australis created by Quirós loomed ever larger. La Austrialia del Espíritu Santo, with its perfect tropical climate, its abundant and splendid fruits, its docile, well-proportioned inhabitants, would form the northeast boundary of Terra Australis in the imaginative, optimistic geography of the age.

In Britain the synthesis of Terra Australis with La Austrialia del Espíritu Santo had been achieved in the wake of Dampier's expeditions by the cartographer of his voyages, Herman Moll. In 1717 he divided *Terra Australis Incognita* into New Holland, Carpentaria, Terra Austral del Spiritu Santo, and Solomon's Islands to the north, and Diemen's Land and New Zealand to the south. In Moll's glowing account of the largely unknown lands lying within these boundaries, he relies upon Quirós's vision of Terra Australis, rather than Dampier's negative assessment of New Holland.[58]

In France the dismal picture of New Holland was transformed by geographers who 'drew on the Quirós discovery of 1606 to suggest the presence of rich countries inside the great oval traced by Tasman on his voyage of 1642–3'.[59] In Nicolas Sanson's world map of 1678 (see figure 43) the 'Terre de Quir' lies to the east of 'Nouvelle Hollande' and directly south of the Solomon Islands. The leading French cartographer of the early eighteenth century, Guillaume de l'Isle, continued along the lines traced by his predecessor. His 'Hémisphère Méridional' of 1714 incorporates Espíritu Santo, greater than an island but not quite a continent, within the contours of the 'Terres Australes'.[60]

By the mid-eighteenth century the luminous Austrialia del Espíritu Santo was inextricably linked to its direct opposite, New Holland, in the minds of European geographers. The *Complete System of Geography* (1747), published under the name of Emanuel Bowen, noted that 'it is very probable, that New Guiney, New-Holland, Van Diemen's Land, and the Land of the Holy Ghost, the Country discovered by de Quiros, make all together one great Continent, separated from New-Zealand by a Streight'.[61] In the caption to his 'Complete Map of the Southern Continent', published in John Campbell's revision of John Harris's collection of voyages (figure 72),[62] Bowen states unequivocally that 'the Country discovered by Ferdinand de Quiros lies according to his description on the East Side of this Continent directly Opposite to Carpentaria'. As the caption indicates, Bowen's map was in turn

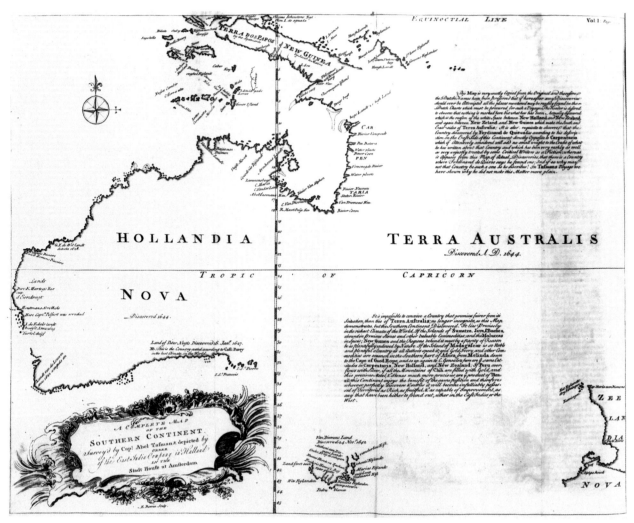

72 Emanuel Bowen, *A Complete Map of the Southern Continent*, 1744, engraving from J. Campbell/John Harris, *Navigantium atque Itinerarium Bibliotheca*, Mitchell Library, State Library of New South Wales

based upon the newly restored great floor map in the Amsterdam Town Hall. Whereas the original seventeenth-century version announced Tasman's discoveries to the world, the revised map of 1742–47, in conformity with new geographical concepts, placed Espíritu Santo firmly on the northeast portion of Terra Australis, linked to Van Diemen's Land by an imaginary coastline.[63]

The enticing image of Quirós's utopian world constituted the central focus of Charles de Brosses's *Histoire des Navigations aux Terres Australes* (1756).[64] Like his contemporaries, de Brosses was convinced that the extensive, hitherto undiscovered Terra Australis would supply the world with a vast quantity of riches in the form of animals, medicinal plants, and mineral resources. And, whereas in the text the nature of the unknown world is left ambiguous (a continent or a series of islands), the illustrative map by Robert de Vaugondy follows contemporary thought by placing Espíritu Santo on the imaginary east coast of Terra Australis (figure 73).[65]

The optimistic reports of John Campbell and Charles de Brosses may have encouraged the VOC to make one last effort. In 1756 an expedition of Jean Etienne Gonzal and Lavienne Lodewijk van Aaschens explored eastern

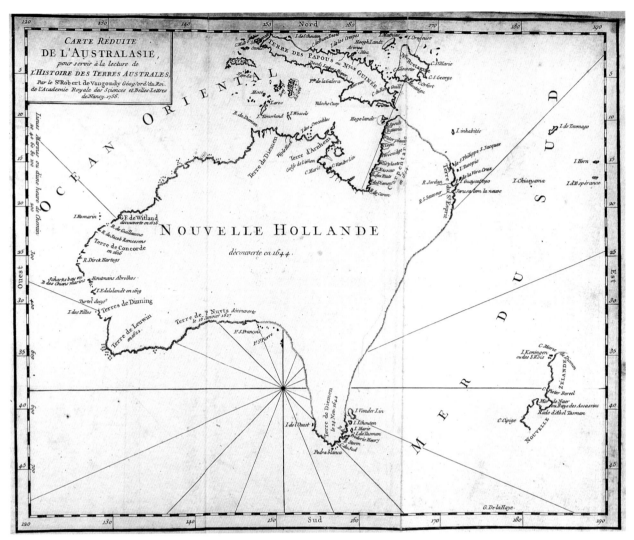

73 Robert de Vangondy, *Australasia*, 1756, engraved map from Charles de Brosses, *Histoire des navigations aux terres australes*, by permission of British Library

Arnhem Land and the Gulf of Carpentaria. In their report the two men noted that 'On the whole the country looked promising enough, and when cultivated would prove very fertile'.[66] In the course of the voyage additional 'rarities' from New Holland were obtained; two Aborigines were taken captive, and a small canoe was sent to Amsterdam by the governor-general in Batavia.[67] If Dutch interest in the Southland was rekindled by these hopeful accounts, the dwindling resources of their declining empire discouraged any further efforts.

Epilogue:
Dutch Images of the
Southland and the
Voyage of the *Endeavour*

13

The works of John Campbell and Charles de Brosses were intended to encourage their respective governments to launch new initiatives to extract the hidden wealth which had supposedly eluded the Dutch. In the following decades the principal exponent of Australian exploration, Alexander Dalrymple, campaigned ceaselessly on behalf of new, large-scale voyages of exploration to discover the southern continent. His efforts encouraged the Admiralty and the Royal Society to undertake the first of three great expeditions in the Pacific, commanded by Captain James Cook.[1]

Prior to the departure of Cook's *Endeavour* in 1768, Dalrymple presented a special advance copy of his illustrated anthology of voyages, *An Account of the Discoveries made in the South Pacifick Ocean Previous to 1764* to Joseph Banks (printed in 1767, the work was not published until the following year).[2] In a chart accompanying the text (figure 74), Dalrymple traced the vague outlines of 'Tierra del Esp.e Santo or Manicola' to the east of New Holland.[3] The 'Bay of St. Philip and St. Jago' and the port of Vera Cruz founded by Quirós are clearly delineated; to the east and west all is uncertainty. Not far from the eastern perimeter of Dalrymple's Espíritu Santo are the islands discovered by le Maire and Tasman in Futuna and Tonga,

74 Alexander Dalrymple, *Chart of the South Pacifick Ocean*, 1767, engraving from A. Dalrymple, *An Account of the Discoveries made in the South Pacifick Ocean Previous to 1764*, by permission of British Library

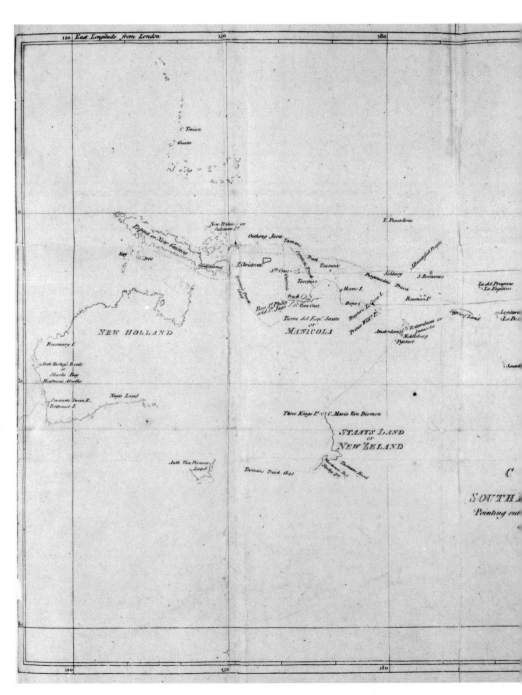

islands which must have seemed far removed from the wretched coasts of New Holland, New Guinea, and New Zealand in terms of their topography, climate and, above all, their inhabitants.

The depictions of the Tongans reproduced in Dalrymple's work and examined by Banks aboard the *Endeavour* were endowed with a rococo grace and beauty which coincided with the positive image of Espíritu Santo. As we have seen, this image, based upon the memorials of Quirós, superseded in part the negative impression of New Holland in the eighteenth century. Dalrymple's illustrations derived ultimately from Isaac Gilsemans; they are very different, however, from the prosaic seventeenth-century originals. For

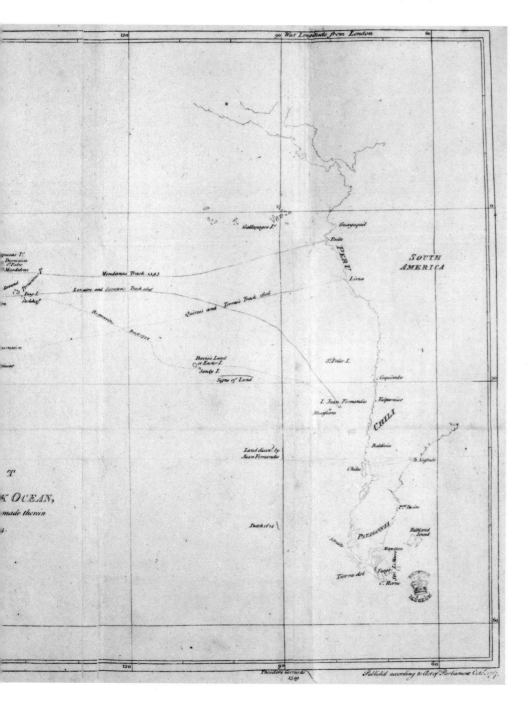

Banks and his artists, the idealized vision of the South Pacific evoked by these plates would have appeared to coincide with what they actually encountered in Tahiti.

The plates in Dalrymple's *Account* constituted a portion of the very limited information from Dutch sources which was accessible to Banks and Cook. Banks himself lamented the lack of reliable data in his *Endeavour* journal: 'Thus much for Tasman: it were much to be wished however that we had a fuller account of his voyage than that publish'd by Dirk Rembranse which seems no more than a short extract'.[4]

The brief account of Tasman's voyage referred to by Banks is an abridged English version of *Eeinige Oefeningen* by Dirk Rembrandtszoon van Nierop (Amsterdam 1674), printed in John Narborough's *Account of several late Voyages and Discoveries* (London 1694–1711). Van Nierop's text was supplemented by the condensed account by Dalrymple, who extracted both words and images from François Valentijn's *Oud en Nieuw Oost-Indiën* (1724–26), the earliest comprehensive report on the voyage. At the conclusion of his brief synopsis of Tasman's expedition, Dalrymple observes that:

75 After Isaac Gilsemans, *Natives of Tongatapu*, 1705, engraving from Nicolaas Witsen, *Noord en Oost Tartarye*, Mitchell Library, State Library of New South Wales

The cuts Valentyn has published of Tasman's voyage compensate, in some measure, for the very brief relation of the journal, which does not even mention the complexion of the natives of Amsterdam and Rotterdam, and has omitted to describe the embarkations, &c. of the Indians.[5]

Het Eylant Rotterdam inde Zuyt-zee met syn Inwoenders na hetleven afgemaelt beneffens een Vaertuig aldaer.

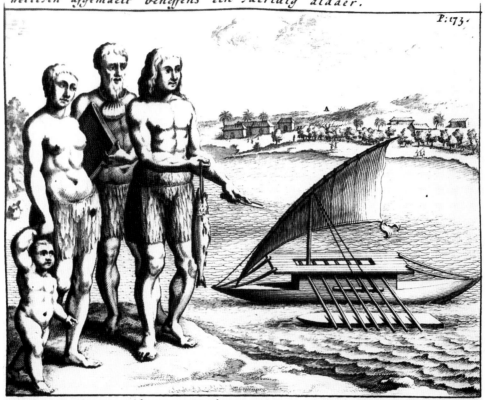

P: 173.

De Man heeft een parlemoere schulp om dehals en eenstuk geweven Matten of Riet inde hant By A. iseen ronde Water poel daer Eenden swemmen.

Vaertuig van Nova gunea byde voor-Eylanden Iamna en Medemo naet leven afgemaelt Op een plaets by A. Tasman int iaer 1643. genaemt, Cornelis Witsens Reede, na de naem des Vaders van den Schriver deses werks, Dit Vaartuis heeft een Vlerk.

76 After Isaac Gilsemans, *Natives of Nomuka and Tabar Island*, 1705, engraving from Nicolaas Witsen, *Noord en Oost Tartarye*, Mitchell Library, State Library of New South Wales

Although Dalrymple provides only a few details from what was in fact a relatively extensive account of Tasman's journey,[6] he faithfully reproduces the illustrations published by Valentijn. Far removed from Gilsemans's originals, these plates served as the only pictorial guide for Banks and his companions in their initial encounters with South Pacific people.

The progressive transformation of Gilsemans's natives commenced in 1705 with the initial publication of the pictures in Nicolaas Witsen's *Noord en Oost Tartarye*, a work apparently unknown to Dalrymple, Banks, and Cook. Having discovered the original drawings in the Dutch East India Company archives, Witsen undertook the task of bringing them to light. As Gilsemans's distorted anatomy, perspective, and proportions were unacceptable to his trained artist's eye, he was compelled to take considerable liberties with the formal aspects of the figures. In the plates (figures 75 and 76) the men and women of Polynesia have become more noble; however, details of ethnographic significance – dress, implements, ornaments – remain unaltered.

The engravings published by Valentijn and reprinted by Dalrymple carry the process of idealization a step further. Gilsemans's painstakingly rendered Tongans have been completely transformed into 'soft' primitives (figures 77 and 78). The female figures in particular are imbued with a certain rococo charm which is absent in Witsen's classical images. On the other hand, the 'authentic' content of the originals has been reduced; the bark mat borne by the central male figure on Nomuka or Rotterdam (figure 78) now takes the form of a small book carried by his female companion.

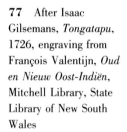

77   After Isaac Gilsemans, *Tongatapu*, 1726, engraving from François Valentijn, *Oud en Nieuw Oost-Indiën*, Mitchell Library, State Library of New South Wales

78 After Isaac Gilsemans, *Nomuka*, 1767, engraving from Alexander Dalrymple, *An Account of the Discoveries made in the South Pacifick Ocean Previous to 1764*, Mitchell Library, State Library of New South Wales

Just as the Tongans drawn by Gilsemans were transformed into 'soft' primitives, the less attractive Maoris of New Zealand were altered into stereotypical 'hard' primitives. In Valentijn's and Dalrymple's plates the squat, grim-looking Maoris have become powerful, well-proportioned savages – formidable adversaries indeed (figure 79).

It was the classicizing, eighteenth-century revision of Gilsemans's images of Pacific people that was carried aboard the *Endeavour*. These pictures, with all their faults, were directly consulted by Banks. In the aftermath of a violent encounter with the Maoris – precisely the sort of tragic incident which both Tasman and Cook wished to avoid in the course of their voyages – Banks carefully examined the body of a 'cheif' killed by the British marines:

> he was coverd with a fine cloth of a manufacture totally new to us, it was tied on exactly as represented in Mr Dalrymple's book, p. 63 [our figure 79]; his hair was also tied in a knot on the top of his head but no feather stuck in it; his complexion brown but not very dark.[7]

In the course of the encounter between the British and the Maoris in Ship Cove, immortalized by Sydney Parkinson's drawings (figure 80), Banks would once again turn to his copy of Dalrymple to confirm what his eyes could see:

> The men in these boats were dressed much as they were represented in Tasmans [that is Dalrymple's] figure, that is 2 corners of the cloth were passed over their shoulders and fastened to the rest of it just below their breast, but few or none had feathers in their hair.[8]

79 After Isaac Gilsemans, *Natives of New Zealand in Golden Bay*, 1767, engraving from Alexander Dalrymple, *An Account of the Discoveries made in the South Pacifick Ocean Previous to 1764*, Mitchell Library, State Library of New South Wales

80 Sydney Parkinson, *New Zealand War Canoe bidding defiance to the Ship*, 1770, pen and wash drawing, by permission of British Library

The powerfully built Maori warriors in Dalrymple's plate after Valentijn may well have served as a point of departure for Parkinson's studies, save for one significant detail. The observations by Banks and his artist regarding the presence, or absence, of plumed decoration paralleled those made on the spot by Gilsemans 126 years earlier. As (presumably) few or none of the Maoris observed were adorned in this manner, Gilsemans may have simply omitted the feathers from his drawing; Tasman's journal explicitly mentions this detail, however. They were, therefore, inserted in 1726 by Valentijn in a reworking of an illustration copied directly from the set by Gilsemans in order to produce a 'correct' image – that is, one which corresponded literally to Tasman's account. The details, inserted in pen, presumably by Valentijn himself, are readily visible on this sheet (figure 81).[9] Valentijn's revision served, in turn, as the model for the plate in Dalrymple's book which Banks consulted.

Like his eighteenth-century counterpart, Sydney Parkinson, Tasman's artist attempted to draw what he actually saw; but, over time – as was also the case with the pictorial record of Cook's voyages – the widely disseminated published images would come to differ considerably from the original, first-hand graphic depictions. Each generation of explorer-artists was, therefore, compelled to rediscover the unknown for themselves. The evidence acquired in past generations was no longer available in its original form; radically transformed, it now served to propagate the myth of a powerful, imposing but terrible race of warriors.

81 After Isaac Gilsemans, *Natives of New Zealand in Golden Bay*, 1643 (reworked 1726), MS., Algemeen Rijksarchief, The Hague

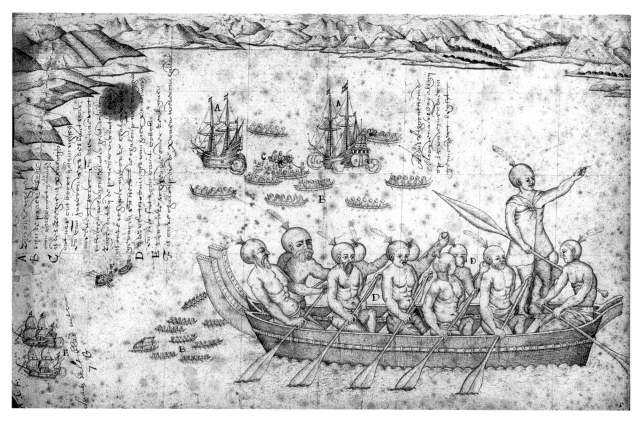

Banks was very much aware of his lack of precise details regarding Tasman's voyages. In 1776 he attempted to correct this oversight by commissioning an English translation of the Dutch explorer's journal, although this remained unpublished.[10] In other respects his knowledge of Dutch discoveries in the Southland was limited, as a passage from his Australian journal suggests:

> Quadrupeds we saw but few and were able to catch a few of them. The largest was calld by the natives Kangooroo. It is different from any European and indeed any animal I have heard or read of except the Gerbua of Egypt, which is not larger than a rat when this is as large as a midling Lamb ...[11]

Banks had either not seen, or could not recall the image of the wallaby illustrated in Cornelis de Bruijn's *Reizen* (figure 71), published in English translation in 1737. Nor had he any knowledge of the 'filanders' preserved in Nicolaas Witsen's cabinet. Conceivably, all traces of this family of animals had vanished from European museums by the late eighteenth century. Certainly, the image of the Southland in late seventeenth-century Holland, which was fragmentary at best, had faded considerably in the course of time. Contrary to what we may suppose, it was not transmitted to the British explorers who sailed for the Pacific in 1768.

The initial voyage of Captain Cook, together with the voyages of his contemporary, Bougainville, marked the virtual disappearance of Terra Australis from the maps of the world. The charting of Pacific waters undertaken by the British navigator and Bougainville brought an end to the ancient dreams of vast, rich lands, waiting to be discovered in the southern hemisphere. When Bougainville arrived in Espíritu Santo, his initial optimism quickly receded before the reality; 'la terre australe du Sant-Esprit' was nothing more than an archipelago, transformed into a continent by the romantic imagination of its Portuguese discoverer.[12]

In the years following the publication of Bougainville's *Voyage autour du monde* (Paris 1771) and John Hawkesworth's edition of Cook's first voyage (London 1773), what remained of Terra Australis 'decomposed' into its 'component parts' – Australia, New Zealand, New Guinea, the Pacific islands, the Antarctic. At the same time, textual and visual impressions of Terra Australis and its natural and human environments – exemplified by a barren and savage New Holland/New Guinea on the one hand, a luxuriant and alluring Espíritu Santo on the other – would inspire parallel visions in New South Wales and Tahiti. Created in the sixteenth and seventeenth centuries from a curious mixture of precise observation and mythmaking, re-elaborated in the Enlightenment, the contradictory image of Australia, New Guinea, and the South Pacific would persist for decades to come. Its legacy is still with us today.

Conclusion

14

$\mathbf{I}$n this essay I have attempted to describe the Western vision of a southern world before it was 'discovered' and delineated by Captain Cook and his successors. Prior to Cook, the image of lands lying far to the south of the equator was based to a considerable degree upon direct observation. I have discussed the various ways in which the visual arts played a role in the complex process of discovery in the southern hemisphere, as elsewhere in the world. The marriage of science and art, an essential factor in this development, took place long before Cook set sail on the *Endeavour*;

however, the two disciplines had not yet been forged as instruments of the national state and its institutions. The state-financed scientific voyages of the eighteenth century, facilitated by important advances in navigation and hygiene, created new opportunities which had not previously existed.

The merger of art and Enlightenment science in the eighteenth century, however fruitful, constituted a loss as well. Whoever examines first-hand the vignettes on early French or Dutch maps, the vibrant images of the bird of paradise from the sixteenth century, or the earliest views of the Australian coast, will, I believe, be struck by a certain freshness and intensity which is absent from studies of a later time. My principal intention, however, has not been to establish criteria of judgement, aesthetic or otherwise, but to describe the context of historical change. Although the positive and negative images of the South Pacific which emerged at the end of the eighteenth century would have a lasting impact upon later generations, they developed within a distinct intellectual and cultural environment. My main purpose has been to delineate a sequence of events and processes which are to a certain extent autonomous and discontinuous. I have attempted to describe the manner in which images of the southern world emerged at different moments under particular circumstances in the histories of collecting, patronage, exploration, cartography, and so on.

The discontinuous image-making process was, in turn, paralleled by the course of the history of Pacific exploration. Each period, each national effort remained distinct; and whereas important exchanges and borrowings occurred continuously, there was no steady progress from darkness to enlightenment. Written and graphic records were lost, concealed, or radically transformed. Precise depictions of human and animal forms were employed to create new myths. It is this remarkable series of oscillations between diffusion and concealment, between the real and the imaginary, which constitutes the intriguing vision of Terra Australis.

Notes

Chapter 1

1 This work is a greatly expanded version of my article, 'Terra Australis: Art and Exploration 1500–1768', in William Eisler and Bernard Smith (eds), *Terra Australis: The Furthest Shore*, exhibition catalogue (Sydney 1988), pp. 15–34.
2 Smith, *European Vision*, p. 6.
3 See, however, his essay 'Art in the Service of Science and Travel' in a new collection of his articles, *Imagining the Pacific in the Wake of the Cook Voyages* (Melbourne 1992), pp. 1–40, which includes a survey of the subject prior to the eighteenth century.
4 Smith, *European Vision*, p. v.
5 ibid. p. 4.
6 ibid. p. 6.
7 ibid. p. 7.
8 ibid. pp. 232–40.
9 See J. E. Hoffman, 'Nascent New Holland: Frontier Client to the Netherlands Indian Ocean State', *International Conference on Indian Ocean Studies* (Perth 1979), pp. 1–37.

Chapter 2

1 This chapter is based principally upon Numa Broc, 'De l'antichtone à l'antarctique' in *Cartes et figures de la terre*, exhibition catalogue (Paris 1980), pp. 136–47. See also Helen Wallis, 'Visions of Terra Australis in the Middle Ages and Renaissance', in William Eisler and Bernard Smith (eds), *Terra Australis: The Furthest Shore*, exhibition catalogue (Sydney 1988), pp. 35–38, and Glyndwr Williams and Alan Frost, 'Terra Australis: Theory and Speculation' in Williams and Frost (eds), *Terra Australis to Australia* (Melbourne 1988), pp. 1–37. The classic work is Armand Rainaud, *Le Continent Austral: Hypothèses et Découvertes* (Paris 1893).
2 The manuscript is preserved in the cathedral of Osma. See T. Rojo Orcajo, 'El Beato de la Catedral de Osma', in *Art Studies* (Cambridge Mass. 1931), pp. 100–56; A. Balil, 'El códice de Beato de Liébana en Burgo de Osma y las representaciones de faros en el mismo', *Celtiberia* 55 (1978), pp. 7–12; *Los Beatos*, exhibition catalogue (Brussels 1985), cat. n.3.

Chapter 3

1 Quoted in Numa Broc, 'De l'antichtone à l'antarctique', in *Cartes et figures de la terre* exhibition catalogue (Paris 1980), p. 141.

2 The large, brightly coloured Brazilian macaws represented on the Cantino map are clearly distinguished from the small green parrots of Africa. See Hugh Honour, 'Science and Exoticism: The European Artist and the Non-European World before Johan Maurits', in Ernst van den Boogaart, H. R. Hoetink, and P. J. P. Whitehead (eds), *Johan Maurits van Nassau-Siegen (1604–1679). A Humanist Prince in Europe and Brazil* (The Hague 1979), p. 279.

3 Helen Wallis, 'The Cartography of Drake's Voyage', in Norman J. Thrower (ed.), *Sir Francis Drake and the Famous Voyage, 1577–1580. Essays Commemorating the quadricentennial of Drake's circumnavigation of the Earth* (Berkeley, Los Angeles and London 1984), p. 124.

4 See Armando Cortesão (ed.), *The Suma Oriental of Tomé Pires and the Book of Francisco Rodrigues* 2 vols (London 1944).

5   That day [14 July] at 10 o'clock in the morning we saw in the northeast
       some thick and furled clouds from the midst of which there emerged a
       form like an elephant's trunk and known to sailors as a waterspout,
       moving down to the sea; around this trunk or waterspout there was
       nothing to obstruct our view, such as mist or thick fog. The part of this
       spout attached to the clouds drifted away on one side and on the other
       formed a head which as it travelled down to the sea took on a plump
       and rounded shape; the part which touched the sea raised a seething
       mass of boiling waters around it and, as those of us who saw it observed,
       it appeared to suck in water and to carry it upwards through its spout;
       this might have lasted some fifteen minutes and we would have been
       little more than half a league away from it; and as its intensity
       decreased it was followed by heavy rain and thunder. The way the spout
       started to form was through the appearance in the sea of much vapour
       and turbulently boiling waters, the size of a ship which, before we could
       recite two credos, had grown and was moving upwards until it reached
       the sky, as we have attempted to show in this drawing of a waterspout
       where the water is seen rising up to the clouds.

    Armando Cortesão and Luís de Albuquerque (eds), *Obras completas de João de Castro* vol. 1 (Lisbon 1968), pp. 228–29. I wish to thank His Excellency, Mr I. Rebello de Andrade, Ambassador of Portugal to Australia, for providing the English translation of de Castro's text.

6 Leonard Bacon (ed. and trans.), *The Lusiads of Luiz de Camões* (New York 1950), pp. 179–80.

7 Smith, *European Vision and the South Pacific 1768–1850. A Study in the History of Art and Ideas* (Oxford 1960), pp. 48–50.

8 On Leonardo the basic reference is Carlo Pedretti (ed.), *The Drawings and Miscellaneous Papers of Leonardo da Vinci ... at Windsor Castle* (London and New York 1981). On Dürer and the development of natural history illustration see Fritz Koreny, *Albrecht Dürer und die Tier- und Pflanzenstudien der Renaissance*, exhibition catalogue (Munich 1985).

9   For the study of the Irishmen (Berlin, Staatliche Museen Preussischer Kulturbesitz) see *Albert Dürer aux Pays-Bas*, exhibition catalogue (Brussels 1977), p. 76 no.83. For the portrait of the African servant (Florence, Uffizi) see *Albrecht Dürer 1471–1971*, exhibition catalogue (Munich 1971), p. 294 no.543.

10 On Burgkmair's woodcuts and works derived from them, in particular a splendid, early sixteenth-century tapestry, see Götz Pochat, ' "Triumphus Regis Gosci sive Gutschmin". Exoticism in French Renaissance Tapestry', *Gazette des Beaux Arts* 82 (1973), pp. 305–10.

11 The drawing was executed in ink as a marginal decoration for the Book of Hours of Emperor Maximilian I. See William C. Sturtevant, 'First Visual Images of Native America', in Fredi Chiapelli (ed.), *First Images of America* vol. I (Berkeley, Los Angeles and London 1976), p. 423.

12 For Dürer's frequently cited remarks concerning the Mexican treasures displayed at the court of Charles V in Brussels (1520) see Hugh Honour, *The New Golden Land: European Images of America from the Discoveries to the Present Time* (New York 1975), p. 28.

Chapter 4

1   Antonio Pigafetta, *Il primo viaggio intorno al mondo* (Rome 1989).

2   O. H. K. Spate, *The Spanish Lake (The Pacific since Magellan, I)* (Canberra 1979), p. 57.

3   Helen Wallis, 'Java la Grande: The Enigma of the Dieppe Maps', in Williams and Frost (eds), *Terra Australis to Australia* (Melbourne 1988), p. 40.

4   ibid. pp. 40–41. The manuscript account of the expedition was published in C. Schefer (ed.), *Le Discours de la navigation de Jean et Raoul Parmentier* (Paris 1883).

5   Wallis, 'Java la Grande', pp. 43–44.

6   Cited and translated in ibid. pp. 50–51.

7   See H. Wallis (ed.), *The Maps and Text of the Boke of Idrography presented by Jean Rotz to Henry VIII, 1542* (Oxford 1981).

8   ibid. p. 80.

9   On the voyage of Rotz to Brazil see Wallis, 'Java la Grande', pp. 49–50. On the importance of his Brazilian drawings as ethnographic records see William C. Sturtevant, 'First Visual Images of Native America, in Fredi Chiapelli (ed.), *First Images of America* vol. I (Berkeley, Los Angeles and London 1976), p. 427.

10 See the discussion by W. Sturtevant in Wallis, *Boke of Idrography*, pp. 67–68.

11 Wallis, 'Java la Grande', p. 66.

12 Pigafetta describes these animals as having the head and large ears of a mule, the neck and body of a camel, and the tail of a horse (in *Il primo viaggio*, p. 91).

13 Possibly the earliest representation of cannibalism in America is a Portuguese manuscript map of ca. 1502 in the Bayerische Staatbibliothek, Munich. In the Brazilian portion of the map a white man skewered on a spit is roasted by

Brazilian Indians. More interesting ethnographically is a woodcut of Tupinimba cannibals from Brazil, accompanied by a text derived from a German translation of a Vespucci letter (ca. 1505). The feather ornaments worn by the Indians appear to be at least partially accurate representations (Sturtevant, 'First Visual Images', p. 420).

14 Wilma George, *Animals and Maps* (London 1969) pp. 176–79, cited in Wallis, 'Java la Grande', p. 67.

15 Regarding the presence of wallabies in European collections prior to Cook's voyage to Australia, see chapter 11. Concerning specimens of fruit bats and cassowaries, see Wilma George, 'Alive or Dead: Zoological Collections in the Seventeenth Century', in Oliver Impey and Arthur MacGregor (eds), *The Origins of Museums: The Cabinet of Curiosities in Sixteenth and Seventeenth Century Europe* (Oxford 1985) pp. 179–85.

16 Wallis, 'Java la Grande', p. 67.

17 Armand Rainaud, *Le Continent austral: Hypothèses et Découvertes* (Paris 1893), pp. 274–75.

18 The basic study on the European discovery of the bird of paradise is Erwin Stresemann, 'Die Entdeckungsgeschichte der Paradiesvögel', *Journal für Ornithologie* 95 n.3/4 (1954), pp. 263–91. For the iconography of the bird in the sixteenth century see Fritz Koreny, *Albrecht Dürer und die Tier- und Pflanzenstudien der Renaissance*, exhibition catalogue (Munich 1985), pp. 100–11.

19 Koreny, *Dürer*, cat. no.30, pp. 102–103.

20 Maximilianus Transsylvanus, *Epistola ... de ... novissima Hispanorum in Orientem navigatione* (Rome 1523), quoted in Stresemann, 'Die Entdeckungsgeschichte', p. 264.

21 Pigafetta, *Il primo viaggio*, p. 176.

22 See Stresemann, 'Die Entdeckungsgeschichte', pp. 264–65. The question as to whether Baldung's drawing depicts one of the five birds brought to Europe by the Magellan expedition, as Koreny has argued, hinges in part upon the condition of the specimen. The drawing would seem to suggest that the animal was without legs and wings; it appears however that del Cano's specimens possessed legs but not wings. At least this is suggested in Stresemann's article, upon which Koreny's account depends; Pigafetta, the only eyewitness cited by Stresemann, describes the birds from the *Victoria* in this manner. Koreny's statement that the five birds arrived in Seville with their feet removed (p. 100) would appear to be unsubstantiated.

23 Stresemann, 'Die Entdeckungsgeschichte', p. 265.

24 Cardano, *De Subtilitate libri XXI* (Nuremberg 1550), p. 239, cited in Stresemann, 'Die Entdeckungsgeschichte', p. 265.

25 (Paris 1555), pp. 329–30, cited in Stresemann, 'Die Entdeckungsgeschichte', pp. 265–66.

26 *La historia de las Indias* (Saragossa 1552), p. 546, cited in Stresemann, 'Die Entdeckungsgeschichte', p. 266.

27 ... *Historiae Animalium Liber III qui est de Avium natura* (Zürich 1555), pp. 611–14, cited in Stresemann, 'Die Entdeckungsgeschichte', p. 266 (German transl. of *Historiae: Vogelbuch*, Zürich 1557).

28 *Musaeum Franc. Calceolarii Veronensis ...* (Verona 1584), cited in Stresemann, 'Die Entdeckungsgeschichte', p. 267.

29 Koreny, *Dürer*, p. 108; cat. no.33 (Dresden) is thought to be a watercolour sketch for the left-hand side of the drawing in Copenhagen.

30 The possibility that the Copenhagen drawing may bear some relationship to the work of Jacopo Ligozzi, author of numerous studies of plants and animals executed on behalf of the Medici court, was suggested to me by Erik Fischer, curator of the Department of Prints and Drawings, the Royal Museum of Fine Arts, Copenhagen.

31 Stresemann, 'Die Entdeckungsgeschichte', pp. 268–69. On the voyage of Van Heemskerck and its relationship to the work of Carolus Clusius see J. Heniger, 'De eerste Nederlandse wetenschappelijke expeditie naar Oost-Indië, 1599–1601', *Leidse Jaarboekje* (1973), pp. 27–49.

32 Stresemann, 'Die Entdeckungsgeschichte', pp. 279–80.

33 See Rainaud, *Le Continent Austral*, pp. 312–18.

34 See W. Waterschoot, 'The Title-Page of Ortelius's *Theatrum Orbis Terrarum*', *Quarendo* 9 (1979), pp. 43–68, and Ernst van den Boogaart, 'Europeanen en niet-Europeanen in zestiende-eeuws Nederlands perspectief', *De Gids* 145 (1982), pp. 6–25.

35 Hans Staden's account of his captivity among the Brazilian cannibals, *Wahrhaftige Historia und beschreibung eyner landschafft der Wilden Nacketen Grimmingen Menschfresser Leuthen in der Neuenwelt America Gelegen* (Marburg 1557), was published in Dutch (1558), French (1559), and Latin (1592).

36 See Waterschoot, 'Title-page', pp. 51–55.

37 The account of the coastal fires in the Strait is derived from Maximilianus Transsylvanus. It is the latter, and not Pigafetta, who informs us that the explorers saw fires on the coast, indicating that they had been observed by the natives. This account appears for the first time in Maximilianus's *De Moluccis insulis* (Basel 1555), p. 529. See Waterschoot, 'Title-Page', pp. 55–56.

38 This translation is taken from Waterschoot, 'Title-page', pp. 61–62.

39 Notably the string of bells around her right leg, her club, and the hammock in the background, all of which can be identified with actual Brazilian artefacts.

40 On Plancius see Kees Zandvliet, *De groote waereld in 't kleen geschildert. Nederlandse kartografie tussen de middeleeuwen en die industriële revolutie* (Alphen aan den Rijn 1985), p. 33; M. Destombes, *La mappemonde de Petrus Plancius* (Hanoi 1944); J. Keuning, *Petrus Plancius, theoloog en geograaf, 1552–1622* (Amsterdam 1946).

41 Plancius's figure of Asia, conforming with the contemporary image of this continent, is elaborately dressed, wearing a turban, holding a censer in her right hand and a spice branch in the other, with a jewel-box at her feet. In these respects the image corresponds well with contemporary figuration. However, Plancius's figure is shown riding upon the back of a rhinoceros, whereas in general the dromedary is depicted in this role. The rhinoceros is often included as an attribute of Asia, but is more frequently placed in the background. See Sabine Poeschel, *Studien zur Ikonographie der Erdteile in der Kunst des 16.–18. Jahrhunderts* (Munich 1985).

42 The iconography of Magellanica has received scant attention in the literature; scholars have mistaken it for a division of America. This error appears in Poeschel, *Erdteile*, pp. 71, 287, and in Jean-Paul Duviols, *L'Amerique espagnole vue et rêvée. Les livres de voyages de Christophe Colomb à Bougainville* (Paris 1985) pp. 80–81.

43 Ernst van den Boogaart, 'The Mythical Symmetry in God's Creation: The Dutch and the Southern Continent 1569–1756', in William Eisler and Bernard Smith (eds), *Terra Australis: The Furthest Shore*, exhibition catalogue (Sydney 1988), pp. 43–50.

Chapter 5

1 I have based my account of the voyages of Mendaña, Quirós, and Torres upon O. H. K. Spate, *The Spanish Lake (The Pacific since Magellan, I)* (Canberra 1979), pp. 119ff., and Roberto Ferrando Pérez's introduction to his edition of Pedro Fernández de Quirós, *Descubrimiento de las regiones austriales* (Madrid 1986).

2 Roberto Ferrando Pérez, 'Un vocabulario inédito de Sarmiento de Gamboa', in *Homenaje a Paul Rivet* vol. 2 (São Paulo 1955).

3 Prado de Tovar's drawings illustrate Torres's account of his expedition (see de Quirós, *Descubrimiento*, pp. 317–27). The text and graphic material, including several maps by Tovar, were sent to Philip III by Torres from Goa in 1613. On the significance of the drawings see E.-T. Hamy, 'Luis Vaës de Torres et Diego Prado y Tovar, explorateurs de la Nouvelle-Guinée (1606–1607) – Étude Géographique et Ethnographique', *Bulletin de géographie historique et descriptive* 22 (1907), pp. 47–72, and R. Ferrando Pérez, 'Zeichnungen von Südsee-Eingeborenen aus dem frühen 17. Jahrhundert', *Zeitschrift für Ethnologie* 79 (1954) pp. 75–81.

4 This discussion of Quirós's vision of Terra Australis is based upon Armand Rainaud, *Le Continent austral: Hypothèses et Découvertes* (Paris 1893), pp. 332ff. The latter employed texts published in Justo Zaragoza (ed.), *Historia del descubrimiento de las regiones austriales hecho por el general Pedro Fernández de Quirós* 3 vols (Madrid 1876–82) – still the basic source on the subject.

5 L. Antoine de Bougainville, *A Voyage round the World*, transl. J. R. Forster (London 1772), p. 249, as quoted in Bernard Smith, *European Vision and the South Pacific 1768–1850. A Study in the History of Art and Ideas* (Oxford 1960), p. 25.

Chapter 6

1 Quoted in Luís Filipe Barreto, *Caminhos do saber no renascimento português. Estudios de história e teoria da cultura* (Lisbon 1986), p. 124.

2 See Germán Somolinos d'Ardois, *Vida y obra de Francisco Hernández* (Mexico City 1960). For an English summary of Hernández's activities see David Goodman, 'Philip II's Patronage of Science and Technology', *The British Journal for the History of Science* 16 (1983), pp. 49–66.

3 Drawings which may be derived from the lost works of Hernández appear in a manuscript in the library of the University of Valencia, the *Enciclopedia de História Natural*, presented by Philip II to the Valencian botanist Honorato Pomar. See J. Miguel Morán and Fernando Checa, *El coleccionismo en España* (Madrid 1985), p. 107 n.4.

4 See Somolinos d'Ardois, *Hernández*, pp. 194ff.

5 Fray José de Sigüenza, *Historia de la orden de San Gerónimo* (1605) (Madrid 1907), p. 590, quoted in Somolinos d'Ardois, *Hernández*, p. 263.

6 See Morán and Checa, *Coleccionismo*, p. 110.

7 Sigüenza, *Historia*, p. 366, quoted in Somolinos d'Ardois, *Hernández*, p. 239.

8 Somolinos d'Ardois, *Hernández*, pp. 239–40.

9 See Bernard Smith, *European Vision and the South Pacific 1768–1850. A Study in the History of Art and Ideas* (Oxford 1960) p. 2, where it is stated that: 'Land-travelling scientists had no hope of competing with the results of a Cook, a Flinders, or a Dumont d'Urville'.

Chapter 7

1 A transcription of the first part of Francis Fletcher's manuscript, describing the voyage through the strait, survives (British Library, Sloane 61). It was executed in 1677 by John Conyers. Fletcher's complete text undoubtedly was the source for the principal account of Drake's voyage, *The World Encompassed* (1628). See Helen Wallis, 'The Cartography of Drake's Voyage', in Norman J. Thrower (ed.), *Sir Francis Drake and the Famous Voyage, 1577–1580. Essays Commemorating the Quadricentennial of Drake's circumnavigation of the Earth* (Berkeley, Los Angeles and London 1984).

2 Wallis, 'Cartography', p. 123.

3 ibid.

4 Bibliothèque Nationale, Paris, Manuscript Anglais 51 (Wallis, 'Cartography', p. 125).

   The Pierpont Morgan Library, New York, possesses a profusely illustrated manuscript entitled *Histoire Naturelle des Indes*, which scholars have associated with Drake (see Verlyn Klinkenborg, *Sir Francis Drake and the Age of Discovery*, exhibition brochure, The Pierpont Morgan Library, New York 1988). The work, dating from the early 1590s, contains sixty-two botanical illustrations, eighty-nine drawings of fish, animals, and birds, as well as forty-three drawings of Indian, Spanish, and slave activities. With two exceptions, all depict places in the West Indies, naming thirty of Drake's regular ports of call – a principal reason for associating the manuscript with the English navigator. One drawing depicts the ruler of Gilolo, an island in the Moluccas, setting out in his canoe to greet Drake; the caption mentions the explorer by name. (Although the text specifically mentions Gilolo, the canoe depicted appears to resemble a vessel from the Caroline Islands. On the types of craft encountered by Drake in the Pacific see William A. Lessa, 'Drake in the South Seas', in Thrower (ed.), *Drake*, pp. 60–77). The other exception represents an Indian of 'Loranbec', probably near present-day South Carolina, hunting a bird with a bow and arrow. Drake visited this area in 1586 while attempting to rescue the English colonists at Roanoke. The manuscript's drawings and text provide an especially interesting account of Indian marriage customs, agriculture, and so on.

5 Wallis, 'Cartography', pp. 125–128. For a discussion of the drawings see *Sir Francis Drake: An Exhibition to commemorate Francis Drake's Voyage around the World 1577–1580*, exhibition catalogue (London 1977).

6 Natural history specimens were also collected on the voyage. These included medicinal plants and other natural and manufactured products, such as sago bread. The specimens were described and illustrated in Carolus Clusius, *Aliquot notae in Garciae aromatum Historiam* ... (Antwerp 1582). This volume constituted the first published work on the voyage.

7 N. M. Penzer (ed.), *The World Encompassed and Analogous Contemporary Documents concerning Sir Francis Drake's Circumnavigation of the World* (London 1926), p. 111.

8 ibid. p.127.

9 ibid. p. 131.

10 See Nathaniel Grew, *Museum Regalis Societatis* (London 1681), pp. 363–64.

11 See Paul Hulton, *The work of Jacques Le Moyne de Morgues, a Huguenot artist in France, Florida and England* (London 1977). An original drawing by le Moyne, the only surviving work by the artist depicting an American subject, is preserved in the New York Public Library.

12 British Library, Department of Manuscripts, Add. MS 38823, ff. 1–8, quoted in Paul Hulton, *America 1585: The Complete Drawings of John White* (Chapel Hill and London 1984), p. 9.

13 Quoted in Hulton, *America 1585*, p. 27.

14 See Hulton, *America 1585*, pp. 17–19.

15 ibid. pl. 71.

16 ibid. fig. 20.

17 ibid. p. 37.

18 White's efforts may be said to parallel the attempts by the sculptor Erasmus Grasser to render the contorted movements and gestures of Morris dancers in his series of polychromed wood figures for the Munich town hall (1480). See Johanna Müller-Meinigen, *Die Moriskentänzer und andere Arbeiten des Erasmus Grasser für das Alte Rathaus in München* (Munich and Zürich 1984).

19 See Bernadette Bucher, *Icon and Conquest: A Structural Analysis of de Bry's 'Great Voyages'* (Chicago and London 1981).

Chapter 8

1 These instructions were published in *Memorie voor de Koopluyden En andere officieren, Waer op sy, in't stellen van haert Rapporten, sullen hebben te letten, omme de Heeren Bewinthebberen, haer Meesters, van alles punctuelijck te onderrichten* (*Atlas van der Hem*, National Library, Vienna, Bd. 39, 2ff).

Chapter 9

1 See Günter Schilder, 'New Holland: The Dutch Discoveries', in Glyndwr Williams and Alan Frost (eds), *Terra Australis to Australia* (Melbourne 1988), pp. 84–86.

2 C. C. Macknight, *The Farthest Coast: A Selection of Writings related to the History of the Northern Coast of Australia* (Melbourne 1969), p. 37.

3 Schilder, 'New Holland', p. 84, fig. 3.1.

4 ibid. For an illustration see Günter Schilder, *Australia Unveiled. The share of Dutch navigators in the discovery of Australia* (Amsterdam 1976), map 23 and pl. IV.

5 Schilder, 'New Holland', pp. 86–88.

6 Van den Boogaart, 'Mythical Symmetry', pp. 44–45. The basic work on the le Maire expedition is W. A. Engelbrecht and P. J. Herwenden (eds), *De Ontdekkingsreis van Jacob le Maire en Willem Cornelisz Schouten* 2 vols (The Hague 1945).

7 Ernst van de Boogaart, 'The Mythical Symmetry in God's Creation: The Dutch and the Southern Continent 1569–1756', in William Eisler and Bernard Smith (eds), *Terra Australis: The Furthest Shore* exhibition catalogue (Sydney 1988), p. 45.

8 See Jacob le Maire, *Oost ende West-Indische Spieghel ...* (Zutphen 1621), pl. 24.

9 ibid. pl. 25.

10 J. A. J. de Villiers (ed. and transl.), *The East and West Indian Mirror* (London 1906), p. 211.

11 De Villiers, *Mirror*, pp. 211-12.

12 ibid. p. 213.

13 ibid. pp. 213–14.

14 See for example the images of witches by Hans Baldung Grien, discussed in Eugenio Battisti, *L'antirinascimento* vol. I (2nd edn, Milan 1989), pp. 171ff. The illustration in le Maire's work and its later transformations into engravings by de Bry is analyzed in Bernadette Bucher, *Icon and Conquest: A Structural Analysis of the Illustrations of de Bry's Great Voyages* (Chicago 1981), pp. 134–36.

15 De Villiers, *Mirror*, pp. 210–11.

16 In de Bry's representation of the dance on Horne Island, which is not derived from le Maire, the women are represented as small girls, dancing before the 'king'. The scene is shifted by de Bry, becoming an episode of the principal feast wherein kava was offered to the Europeans. See Bucher, *Icon and Conquest*, p. 160.

17 De Villiers, *Mirror*, p. 209.

18 ibid. p. 214.

19 On 31 May le Maire wrote concerning the Horne islanders: 'Het schijnt dat dit Volck is van d'eerste Eeuwe, om dat al haer nootdruft hinck aen de Boomen en wies, en de Vis die zy vinghen aten zy rau'. The journal of Schouten also mentions that the natives ate raw fish but adds: 'soo datmen daer by nae nae't leven siet de gulden eeuwe de Poeten van hebben gheschreven'. Engelbrecht and Herwenden, *Ontdekkingsreis* vol. 1, p. 53.

20 Van den Boogaart, 'Mythical Symmetry', p. 45.

21 This account of the voyage of the *Pera* and the *Arnhem* is derived principally from Schilder, 'New Holland', pp. 89–95.

22 Schilder, *Australia Unveiled*, map 36.

23 J. E. Heeres, *The Part Borne by the Dutch in the Discovery of Australia 1606–1756* (Leiden and London 1899), pp. 36, 39–42.

24 Schilder, 'New Holland', p. 91.

25 Schilder, *Australia Unveiled*, map 31.

26 For example the world map of Cornelis Danckerts and Melchior Tavernier (1628), the world map of Hendrik Hondius (1630) and Willem Blaeu's map of the East Indies (1635). However, no printed maps depicted the discoveries in Arnhem Land until after the second voyage of Tasman in 1644. See Schilder, 'New Holland', pp. 94–95.

Chapter 10

1 My discussion of van Diemen's program of exploration in search of precious metals is closely based upon Kees Zandvliet, 'Golden Opportunities in Geopolitics: Cartography and the Dutch East India Company during the Lifetime of Abel Tasman', in William Eisler and Bernard Smith (eds), *Terra Australis: The Furthest Shore* exhibition catalogue (Sydney 1988) pp. 67–84.

2 ibid. p. 75.

3 J. E. Heeres (ed.), *Abel Janszoon Tasman's Journal* (Amsterdam 1898), pp. 134–35.

4 ibid.

5 The paucity of 'authentic' images of the peoples of the South Pacific prior to the Enlightenment should not appear surprising if one considers that very few depictions of this sort survive to give us any indications of the appearance of black Africans from the Cape of Good Hope prior to the mid-eighteenth century. A handful of images by Dutch artists, dating from roughly the same period and including some relatively accurate details of dress, weapons, and so on, were employed repeatedly by publishers in the course of the seventeenth century and early eighteenth century. See the very informative study by Ezio Bassani and Letizia Tedeschi, 'The Image of the Hottentot in the Seventeenth and Eighteenth Centuries', *Journal of the History of Collections* 2 (1990), pp. 157–86.

6 See Andrew Sharp, *The Voyages of Abel Janszoon Tasman* (Oxford 1968), p. 40. A translation of the text is printed on pp. 40–53 of this work.

7 For the historical details concerning Tasman's voyages I have relied upon the excellent synopsis in Günter Schilder, 'New Holland: The Dutch Discoveries', in Glyndwr Williams and Alan Frost (eds), *Terra Australis to Australia* (Melbourne 1988), pp. 97–103.

8 The notches were actually employed by the Tasmanian Aborigines in capturing possums. See Lloyd Robson, *A History of Tasmania* 1 (Melbourne 1983), p. 5.

9 Sharp, *Voyages*, pp. 121–22.

10 ibid. p. 42.

11   The theory that the blackness of Africans was the consequence of God's curse to Ham [condemned after witnessing the drunkenness of his father Noah], though probably known in Holland, was not picked up; indeed, it was no generally accepted opinion that the descendants of Shem, Ham and Japhet still existed as separate peoples. That a black skin was a sign of inner depravity was an association that could occur to Dutchmen whenever they felt particularly threatened by blacks. In the first half of the seventeenth century, it certainly was no part of their equipment of biblical knowledge. Blackness, then, was a most remarkable characteristic of Africans south of the Sahara, but what struck the Dutchmen at least as strongly when they observed African behaviour was their savagery.

Ernst van den Boogaart, 'Colour Prejudice and the Yardstick of Civility: The Initial Dutch Confrontation with Black Africans, 1590–1635', in Robert Ross (ed.), *Racism and Colonialism* (Leiden 1982), p. 46.

    The Dutch attitude towards dark-skinned people in the early seventeenth century as described by van den Boogaart did not differ substantially from the viewpoint of the most important travel writer and editor in the Netherlands in the early eighteenth century, François Valentijn. He refused to accept the theory that black skin constituted a punishment by God for the sins of Ham, and rejected any notion of discrimination on the basis of race. See Jörg Fisch, *Hollands Ruhm in Asien. François Valentyns Vision des niederländischen Imperiums im 18. Jahrhundert* (Stuttgart 1986), pp. 35–37.

12 Sharp, *Voyages*, p. 153.

13 ' ... about noon 32 small canoes and a large ditto furnished with sail, and constructed just as in the Journal of Iacob lamaire in N° is depicted, appeared alongside our ship'. Tasman's reference is to *Oost ende West-Indische Spieghel* (Zutphen 1621), plate 24.

14 Sharp, *Voyages*, p. 155.

15 ibid. p. 157.

16 ibid. p. 163.

17 ibid. p. 164.

18 ibid. p. 168.

19 ibid. p. 154.

20 ibid. p. 170.

21 ibid. p. 171.

22 ibid. p. 45.

23 ibid. p. 155.

24 'The men here had in the breast and shoulders scars a thumb deep and half a finger long' (ibid. p. 47).

25 ibid. p. 43.

26 ibid. p. 44.

27 ibid. p. 47.

28 Regarding these ornaments, see Adrienne Kaeppler, 'Eighteenth century Tonga: new interpretations of Tongan society and material culture at the time of Captain Cook', *Man* 6 (1971), pp. 216–17. A comparable breast ornament is depicted in William Hodges's chalk drawing 'Old man of Amsterdam (Tongatapu)', National Library, Canberra (Rüdiger Joppien and Bernard Smith, *The Art of Captain Cook's Voyages* vol. II: *The Voyage of the 'Resolution' and the 'Adventure' 1772–1775* Melbourne 1985, p. 184, no.2.76).

29 Joppien and Smith, *Voyages* II, p. 182, no.2.74 (Hodges) and ibid. p. 219, no.2.120 (Forster).

30 For example, the craft represented in 'A large Sailing Canoe of the Friendly Islands' in the Mitchell Library, Sydney (Joppien and Smith, *Voyages* II, p. 184, no.2.77) and in 'Tonga Tabu or Amsterdam' in the British Library (ibid. p. 185, no.2.78). Evidently the British were cognizant of these precedents in the course of Cook's second voyage. George Forster noted that the image of a Tongan canoe, observed during le Maire's voyage, was reproduced by Alexander Dalrymple in *A Historical Collection of the Several Voyages and Discoveries in the South Pacific* I (London 1770–71), pp. 17–18 (George Forster, *A Voyage Round the World* I, Dublin 1777, p. 377n).

31 Sharp, *Voyages*, p. 46.

32 According to Peter H. Buck, former director of the Bernice Bishop Museum, Honolulu, the objects (in the National Museum of Denmark, Copenhagen) probably originated in Tonga. Helga Larsen, however, believes that they are more closely related to axes made in Futuna. They may, therefore, have been collected on the voyage of Jacob le Maire. See Helge Larsen, 'Some Ancient Specimens from Western and Central Polynesia', *Ethnographical Studies (Nationalmuseets Skrifter, Etnografisk Raekke)* 1 (1941), pp. 223–50.

33 Sharp, *Voyages*, p. 211.

34 ibid. p. 212.

35 ibid. p. 50.

36 Gilsemans's drawing has been cited as important evidence for the antiquity of the practice and the form of the propeller itself. See H. Peter, 'Haifanggeräte aus Neuirland auf einer Abbildung in Abel Janszoons Tasman's Journal', *Wiener Ethnohistorische Blätter* 23 (1982), pp. 3–23.

37 'Their fish-catching was done strangely. They bound to a cane many small half coconut-husks, assembled in a chain: rattled with this implement on top of the water, to gather the fish' (Sharp, *Voyages*, p. 50).

38 For example, the early eighteenth-century masks discussed in Leopold Schmidt, *Perchtenmasken in Österreich* (Vienna, Cologne, and Graz 1972).

39 Tasman says only that 'their canoes are here very Narrow about one foot broad ... each [man] having with him arrow and bow also darts and harpoons this people was mostly Black and naked having nothing but a small covering before their private parts ...' (Sharp, *Voyages*, pp. 237–38). Haalbos is much more explicit. His observations correspond to many of the details in the drawing: notably the arrangements of the men's hair, their ear and nose ornaments, and the decorations on the prow and stern of the canoe (ibid. p. 51).

40 Günter Schilder, 'New Holland: The Dutch Discoveries', in Glyndwr Williams and Alan Frost (eds), *Terra Australis to Australia* (Melbourne 1988), p. 100.

41 Zandvliet, 'Golden Opportunities', p. 77.

42 Originally thought to date from the period immediately after Tasman's second voyage, the map is now believed to have been executed at the end of the seventeenth century (Günter Schilder, *Australia Unveiled. The share of Dutch navigators in the discovery of Australia*, Amsterdam 1976, map 56).

43 Schilder, 'New Holland', p. 103.

44 See F. Wieringa (ed.), *De wereld volgens Blaeu: Blaeu's wereldkaart op groot formaat uit 1646* (Rotterdam 1986).

45 Zandvliet, 'Golden Opportunities', pp. 79–80.

46 ibid. p. 79.

47 The map (in the Algemeen Rijksarchief, The Hague) is illustrated and described in Kees Zandvliet, 'Johan Maurits and the cartography of Dutch Brazil', in Ernst van den Boogaart, H. R. Hoetink and P. J. P. Whitehead, *Johan Maurits van Nassau-Siegen (1604–1679). A Humanist Prince in Europe and Brazil* (The Hague 1979), p. 514.

48 Zandvliet, 'Golden Opportunities', p. 75, fig. 10.

Chapter 11

1 On Dutch artists working abroad the best survey is Horst Gerson, *Ausbreitung und Nachwirkung der holländischen Malerei des 17. Jahrhunderts* (Haarlem 1942).

2 Early Dutch museums have only recently become a subject of special interest to scholars. The collection of the Dutch physician Bernhard Paludanus, its relationship to the publication of the *Itinerario* of Jan Huygen van Linschoten, and its importance in the formation of Danish museums are discussed in H. D. Scheperlern, 'Naturalienkabinett oder Kunstkammer. Der Sammler Bernhard Paludanus und sein Katalogmanuskript in der Königlichen Bibliothek in Kopenhagen', *Nordelbingen* 50 (1981), pp. 157–82. This very useful article provides a valuable account of the interrelationships between middle-class and princely cabinets. On artists' collections the fundamental study is R. W. Scheller, 'Rembrandt en de encyclopedische kunstkammer', *Oud Holland* 84 (1969), pp. 81–147. See also Willem Walter, 'De V.O.C. en de verzamelaars' in F. M. Wieringa (ed.), *De Verenigde Oostindische Compagnie* [V.O.C.] *in Amsterdam* (Amsterdam 1982), pp. 189–222; Th. H. Lunsingh Scheurleer, 'Early Dutch Cabinets of Curiosities', in Oliver Impey and Arthur MacGregor (eds), *The Origins of Museums: The Cabinet of Curiosities in Sixteenth and Seventeenth Century Europe* (Oxford 1985), pp. 115–20; Ellinoor Bergvelt and Renée Kistemaker (eds), *De wereld binnen handbereik: Nederlandse kunst – en rariteitenverzamelingen, 1585–1735* 2 vols (Zwolle 1992).

3 On this point see Giuseppe Olmi, 'Science-Honour-Metaphor: Italian Cabinets of the Sixteenth and Seventeenth Centuries', in Impey and MacGregor, *The Origins of Museums*, pp. 5–16.

4 Caspar Barlaeus, *Medica Hospes sive descriptio publicae gratulationis, que serenissimam, Augustissimamque Reginam, Mariam de Medicis, excepit senatus populusque Amstelodamensis*, (Amsterdam 1638), pp. 29–34.

5 See Joke van der Aar, 'Het Oost-Indisch Huis', in Wieringa (ed.), *De V.O.C. in Amsterdam*, pp. 35–61.

6 My remarks on the nature of Dutch scientific studies overseas are based largely upon Johannes Heniger, 'Dutch Contributions to the Study of Exotic Natural History in the Seventeenth and Eighteenth Centuries', in William Eisler and Bernard Smith (eds), *Terra Australis: The Furthest Shore*, exhibition catalogue (Sydney 1988) pp. 59–66.

7 The most important publications on the subject of Johan Maurits are Ernst van den Boogaart and F. J. Duparc (eds), *Zo wijd de wereld strekt*, exhibition catalogue (The Hague 1979); Ernst van den Boogaart, H. R. Hoetink, and P. J. P. Whitehead (eds), *Johan Maurits: van Nassau-Siegen (1604–1679). A Humanist Prince in Europe and Brazil* (The Hague 1979); Guido de Werd (ed.), *Soweit der Erdkreis Reicht: Johann Moritz von Nassau-Siegen 1604–1679*, exhibition catalogue (Kleve 1979); P. J. P. Whitehead and M. Boeseman, *A portrait of Dutch 17th century Brazil. Animals, plants and people by the artists of Johan Maurits of Nassau* (Amsterdam, Oxford, and New York 1989).

8 See J. C. Beaglehole (ed.), *The "Endeavour" Journal of Joseph Banks, 1768–1771* I (Sydney 1962), pp. 191–92. The presence of Piso and Marcgraf's work in Banks's shipboard library is indicated in a marginal note to his journal (ibid. p. 178). For a list of books carried aboard the *Endeavour* by Banks see Bernard Smith, 'The Intellectual and Artistic Framework of Pacific Exploration in the Eighteenth Century', in Eisler and Smith (eds), *Terra Australis*, p. 127 n.4.

9 Alpers discusses Eckhout's portraits as 'maps' in her widely discussed work, *The Art of Describing. Dutch Art in the Seventeenth Century* (London 1983).

10 Ernst van den Boogaart, 'Infernal Allies: The Dutch West India Company and the Tarairiu 1630–1654', in van den Boogaart, Hoetink, and Whitehead (eds), *Johan Maurits*, pp. 519–38.

11 They are considered as 'rechte originalia, und im ganzen lande, nirgends nicht mehr zu finden seint' which at the same time 'nach dero gnedigstem belieben selbige in andere ordonantien copijren undt bringen lassen'. See Th. M. Lemmens, 'Die Schenkung an Ludwig XIV. und die Auflösung der brasilianischen Sammlung des Johann Moritz 1652–1679', in de Werd, *Soweit der Erdkreis Reicht*, p. 269.

12 ibid. pp. 271ff.

13 The original French text is quoted in Rüdiger Joppien, 'The Dutch Vision of Brazil: Johan Maurits and his artists', in van den Boogaart, Hoetink, and Whitehead (eds), *Johan Maurits*, p. 326.

14 Lemmens, 'Die Schenkung an Ludwig XIV.', p. 285. See also Joppien, 'The Dutch Vision of Brazil', p. 326 n.164.

15 See Whitehead and Boeseman, *A portrait of Dutch 17th century Brazil*, pp. 109ff. for a detailed description and further references.

16 See Karl Ausserer, 'Der Atlas Blaeu der Wiener National-Bibliothek' in *Beiträge zur historischen Geographie* (Leipzig 1929), pp. 1–40; G. P. Burger, 'De Atlas-Blaeu in de Nationalbibliothek', *Het Boek* 18 (1929), pp. 187–92; F. C. Wieder in *Monumenta Cartografica* vol. 5 (The Hague 1933), pp. 145ff; J. van Bracht, *Vingboons-Atlas. Ten geleide en beschriving van de opgenomen paarten* (Rijkswik 1981), pp. 4ff; H. de la Fontaine-Verwey, 'The Glory of the Blaeu Atlas and the "master colourist"', *Quarendo* 11 (1981), pp. 197–229.

17 The attack by de Vlamingh's forces against the fortress on a hillside near Loki, a village on the Hoamoal Peninsula, was recorded in two drawings by Johan Nessel (Algemeen Rijksarchief). These two images, a rough sketch and a more finished drawing, were the sources for the plate depicting the event in the *Atlas van der Hem*. See Wieder, *Monumenta Cartografica* vol. 5, pp. 172–73.

18 G. F. Hoogewerff (ed.), *De twee reizen van Cosimo de Medici prins van Toscane door de Nederlanden 1667–1669* (Amsterdam 1919), p. 76.

19 This section is based largely upon Heniger, 'Dutch Contributions'.

20 On Linnaeus's extensive botanical and zoological studies in the Netherlands (1735–38) see Heniger, 'Dutch Contributions' *passim*.

21 Piso published a profusely illustrated edition of Bontius's works, *Historiae Naturalis & Medicae Indiae Orientalis Libri Sex* (Amsterdam 1658). One of the woodcuts in this volume depicts the Javanese rhinoceros, perhaps the earliest image of the animal to break from the stereotype of the armour-plated monster created by Dürer in the early sixteenth century. See T. H. Clarke, *The Rhinoceros from Dürer to Stubbs, 1515–1799* (London and New York 1986), p. 41.

22 On Rumphius see H. C. D. de Wit (ed.), *Rumphius Memorial Volume* (Baarn 1959); J. Heniger and P. Smit, 'Louis Ulrike en Linnaeus. Nederlandse bijdragen tot de Linneaanse malacologie', *Corresponentieblad van de Nederlandse Malacologische Verenigung* 224 (1985), pp. 38–46.

23 See J. Heniger, *Hendrik Adriaan van Rheede tot Drakenstein (1636–1691) and Hortus Malabaricus* (Rotterdam and Boston 1986).

24 Parkinson copied forty of the 150 drawings by de Bevere in the collection of Joseph Banks. Both the de Bevere drawings and the Parkinson copies are in the British Museum (Natural History). See Donald Ferguson, 'Joan Gideon Loten, F.R.S., the Naturalist Governor of Ceylon (1752–57), and the Ceylonese Artist de Bevere', *Journal of the Royal Asiatic Society* 19 (1907), pp. 217–71.

25 See K. Meier-Lemgo, *Engelbert Kaempfer: 1651–1716. Seltsames Asien (Amoenitates exoticae)* (Detmold 1933).

26 The manuscript also includes images of a native man and woman. See G. Waterhouse, *Simon van der Stel's Journal of his Expedition to Namaqualand 1685–6* (London 1932).

27 See Theodore W. Pietsch, 'Louis Renard's Fanciful Fishes', *Natural History* 1 (1984), pp. 58–67.

Chapter 12

1 There is no recent comprehensive study on Nicolaas Witsen, a lacuna which I hope to fill. The fundamental work remains the biography by J. F. Gebhard, *Het leven van Mr Nicolaas Witsen (1641–1717)* (2 vols, Utrecht 1882). More recent studies include J. N. Albers, 'Een en ander over Mr. Nicolaas Cornelisz Witsen (1641–1717)', *Nederlands Historien* 13 (1979), pp. 19–24; P. J. A. N. Rietbergen, 'Nicolaas Witsen (1641–1717) between the Dutch East India Company and the Republic of Letters', in Robert Ross and George D. Winius, (eds), *All of one company: the VOC in biographical perspective* (Utrecht 1986), pp. 121–34; M. Peters, 'Nicolaas Witsen and Gijsbert Cuper: Two Seventeenth Century Dutch burgomasters and their Gordian Knot', *Lias* 16 (1989), pp. 111–50; Ellinoor Bergvelt and Renée Kistemaker (eds), *De wereld binnen handbereik: Nederlandse kunst- en rariteitenverzamelingen, 1585–1735* 2 vols (Zwolle 1992), *passim*.

2 On Witsen's voyage to Russia and the drawings he made there see N. Witsen, *Moscovische Reyse 1664–1665*, ed. Th. J. G. Locher and P. de Buck, 2 vols (The Hague 1966). Regarding his map of Tartary see Johannes Keuning, 'Nicolaas Witsen as a cartographer', *Imago Mundi* 11 (1954), pp. 95–110. On Witsen as an artist see G. T. Hart, 'Nicolaas Witsen en zijn voorouders', *Oud Holland* 67 (1952), pp. 74–97. The relationship between Jonas Witsen and Jan Lievens is mentioned in Gary Schwartz, *Rembrandt: his life, his paintings* (Middlesex, New York etc. 1985), p. 318.

3 On the relationship between Leibniz and Witsen see Kurt Müller, 'Gottfried Wilhelm Leibniz und Nicolaas Witsen', *Sitzungsberichte der Deutschen Akademie der Wissenschaften, Klasse für Philosophie und Wirtschaftswissen* (1955), pp. 1–45.

4 Published in Gebhard, *Witsen*, II.

5 Witsen obtained a copy of van der Stel's manuscript account of his expedition to Namaqualand. See K. H. Barnard, 'A Description of the Codex Witsenii in the South African Museum', *Journal of South African Botany* 13 (1947), pp. 1–51.

6 Although Maria Syballa Merian's principal sponsor in Surinam was the van Aerssen van Sommelsdijk family, Witsen's assistance is gratefully acknowledged in the preface to her book. On her work see Gertrud Lendorff, *Maria Syballa Merian (1647–1717). Ihr Leben und Werk* (Basel 1955); *Maria Syballa Merian*, exhibition catalogue (Nuremberg 1967); Elisabeth Rücker, *Maria Syballa Merian* (Bonn 1980).

7 On de Bruijn see W. Blankwaard, 'Cornelis de Bruijn (1652–1719?)', *Historia* 10 (1944), pp. 69–72, and Horst Gerson, *Ausbreitung und Nachwirkung der holländischen Malerei des 17. Jahrhunderts* (Haarlem 1942), p. 539.

8 'His drawings and the engravings made after them were so accurate, that his publication of this monument was employed by Grotefend as late as 1824 to decipher the inscriptions'. (Gerson, *Ausbreitung*, p. 595).

9 Gebhard, *Witsen* II, pp. 350–54.

10 *Catalogus van de uitmuntende en zeer Konst-en Natuurkabinetten ... zeer keurlyk by een vergadert en naargelaten door den Weled. Heer en Mr Nicolaas Witsen ... welke verkocht zullen worden ... den 30 Maarte 1728* (Rijksbureau voor Kunsthistorische Documentatie, The Hague, Lugt n.368).

11 Rietbergen, 'Witsen,' p. 130.

12 ibid. pp. 128–30.

13 See Müller, 'Leibniz und Nicolaas Witsen'.

14 See J. E. Heeres, *The Part Borne by the Dutch in the Discovery of Australia 1606–1756* (Leiden and London 1899), pp. 75–80.

15 See William Eisler and Bernard Smith (eds), *Terra Australis: The Furthest Shore* (Sydney 1988), p. 110, cat. 74.

16 Heeres, *The Part Borne by the Dutch*, p. 81.

17 In his *Noord en Oost Tartarye* (Amsterdam 1705), p. 175.

18 *Catalogus*, part III, p. 16.

19 The factual data on the voyage is derived from Günter Schilder, *Voyage to the Great Southland: Willem de Vlamingh 1696–1697* (Sydney 1985). A brief summary appears in Schilder, 'New Holland: The Dutch Discoveries', in Glyndwr Williams and Alan Frost (eds), *Terra Australis to Australia* (Melbourne 1988), pp. 109–10.

20 Gebhard, *Witsen* II, p. 294.

21 ibid.

22 Schilder, *Voyage*, p. 217.

23 The remaining three drawings depict the islands of Tristan da Cunha, St Paul, and Amsterdam. See Schilder, *Voyage*, pp. 82–89.

24 Rijksmuseum Nederlands Scheepvaart Museum, Amsterdam (Ernst van den Boogaart and F. J. Duparc eds, *Zo wijd de wereld strek*, exhibition catalogue, The Hague 1979, p. 91, cat. nos 75 and 76).

25 Gebhard, *Witsen* II, pp. 299–300.

26 Facsimile in Schilder, *Voyage*.

27 In Jan de Marre and Joannes van Keulen, *De nieuwe Groot Lichtende Zee-Fakkel, Het Sesde Deel, Vertoonende de Zee-Kusten, Eylanden en Havens van Oost-Indien* (Amsterdam 1753).

28 For a summary of Dampier's discoveries see Glyndwr Williams, 'New Holland to New South Wales: The English Approaches' in Williams and Frost (eds), *Terra Australis to Australia*, pp. 117–33.

29 ibid. p. 124.

30 ibid.

31 ibid. p. 125.

32 ibid. p. 133.

33 See Serena K. Marner, 'William Dampier and his Botanical Collection', in Howard Morphy and Elizabeth Edwards (eds), *Australia in Oxford* (Oxford 1988), pp. 1–3; John Mulvaney, 'William Dampier, Ethnography and Elf-stones', *The Artefact* 3 (1978), pp. 151–56.

34 The schematic engraved images of birds and fish are reproduced in Williams, 'New Holland to New South Wales', p. 132, figs 4.11, 4.12.

35 Sedgwick Museum, E.17.7 and E.17.17.

36 Mulvaney, 'Dampier', p. 154.

37 William Dampier, *A Voyage to New Holland*, ed. James Spencer (Gloucester 1981), p. 210.

38 Gebhard, *Witsen* II, p. 363.

39 See P. A. Leupe, *De Reizen der Nederlanders naar het Zuidland of Nieuw-Holland in de 17e en 18e eeuw* (Amsterdam 1868) pp. 185–203; R. H. Major (ed.), *Early Voyages to Terra Australis, now called Australia* (London 1859), pp. 165–73; L. C. D. van Dijk, *Twee Togten naar de Golf van Carpentaria*, (Amsterdam 1859).

40 See Arthur Wichmann, *Entdeckungsgeschichte von Neu-Guinea (bis 1828)* (Leiden 1909), pp. 138–52.

41 VEL 490 (Eisler and Smith, *Terra Australis*, cat. no.81, p. 114). See also P. A. Leupe and J. M. Obreen, *Geschiedzeevaartkundige toelichting betreffende eene kaart van de Geelvinkspaai …* (The Hague 1866).

42 Quoted from de Bruijn, *Travels into Muscovy, Persia and part of the East Indies* (London 1737), p. 89.

43 ibid.

44 Concerning the capture of the Papuans by Weyland and their voyage to the Netherlands see Wichmann, *Entdeckungsgeschichte*, p. 144 n.1.

45 The pictures formed part of Witsen's collection and were catalogued in the auction list under 'Schilderyen en Portraiten' as 'Twee geschilderde Portraiten van de Zuydlanders, die hier voor dezen te zien zyn geweest' (*Catalogus*, part III, p. 14, n.6). Witsen refers to the captives and pictures in his correspondence with Cuper. In a letter of 8 February 1714 he notes that many of the blacks in the Southland have short curly hair (two of whom he had met and conversed with)

whereas others, whose portraits he had commissioned, had long hair: 'Vele der swarten op het Suytlant hebben kort gecrult hajr so als ik er twe heb gesien en gesproken, andere weder lang, waervan de schilderij heb doen maken'. (Gebhard, *Witsen* II, p. 373).

46 Peters, 'Nicolaas Witsen and Gijsbert Cuper', p. 144 n.13.

47 De Bruijn, *Travels*, p. 101.

48 See *Catalogus*, part IV, p. 23, n. 8 ('Een Philander of Bos-rot, met een zak daar de Jongen in en uitlopen') and n.17 ('Een Philander of Bos-rot met zyn Jongen').

49 Williams and Frost, 'Terra Australis: Theory and Speculation', in Williams and Frost (eds) *Terra Australis* p. 17, fig. 1.11.

50 See François Valentijn, *Oud en Nieuw Oost-Indiën* (Dordrecht and Amsterdam 1724–26), vol. II, part 3, pp. 539, 563–64, 566, 571, 576. Voet was the author of many flower pieces as well as a manuscript with illustrations of the insects in his cabinet, 'Nederlansche Insekten naar't Leven naauwkeurig geteekend met derzelver natuurlijke Couleuren en de Beschrijvingen, sowie eine Systematische Naamlijst der torren en kevers' (1725; cited in Claus Nissen, *Die Zoologische Buchillustrationen* I, Stuttgart 1966, p. 419).

51 Witsen, *Tartarye*, pp. 162–63.

52 ibid. p. 163.

53 ibid. p. 174.

54 ibid. pp. 169–70.

55 ibid. p. 174.

56 ibid. p. 163.

57 ibid. p. 175.

58 Williams and Frost, 'Terra Australis: Theory and Speculation', p. 23.

59 ibid. pp. 23, 25.

60 ibid. p. 25 and fig. 1.16.

61 ibid. p. 26.

62 ibid. p. 27, fig. 1.18.

63 Marlies Caron and Ellen Fleurbaay, *Hemel en Aarde in de Burgerzaal* (Amsterdam 1981), p. 11.

64 Williams and Frost, 'Terra Australis: Theory and Speculation', pp. 28–29.

65 ibid. fig. 1.23.

66 C. C. Macknight, *The Farthest Coast: A Selection of Writings related to the History of the Northern Coast of Australia* (Melbourne 1969), pp. 40–47.

67 W. C. H. Robert, *The Dutch Explorations 1605–1756 of the North and Northwest Coasts of Australia* (Amsterdam 1973), pp. 162–163.

Chapter 13

1 Glyndwr Williams and Alan Frost, 'Terra Australis: Theory and Speculation', in Glyndwr Williams and Alan Frost (eds), *Terra Australis to Australia* (Melbourne 1988), pp. 1–37.

2 ibid. p. 32.

3 ibid. p. 35, fig. 1.27.

4 Banks, in J. C. Beaglehole (ed.), *The "Endeavour" Journal of Joseph Banks, 1768–1771* 2 vols (Sydney 1962), p. 2.

5 Alexander Dalrymple, *An Account of the Discoveries made in the South Pacifick Ocean previous to 1764* (London 1768), p. 68.

6 See François Valentijn, *Oud en Nieuw Oost-Indiën* (Dordrecht and Amsterdam 1724–26), vol. 2, part 3, pp. 52–54.

7 Banks, in Beaglehole (ed.), *The "Endeavour" Journal*, p. 400.

8 ibid. p. 453.

9 Günter Schilder, *Australia Unveiled. The share of Dutch navigators in the discovery of Australia* (Amsterdam 1976), p. 140.

10 The translation of a copy of Tasman's journal, by G. C. Woide, was commissioned by Banks in 1776. Both the copy and the translation, neither of which has ever appeared in print, were given to the British Museum by Banks. See Schilder, *Australia Unveiled*, p. 144.

11 Beaglehole (ed.), *The "Endeavour" Journal*, pp. 274–75.

12 Numa Broc, 'De l'antichtone à l'antarctique', in *Cartes et figures de la terre*, exhibition catalogue (Paris 1980), p. 149.

Index